Disrupting The Status Quo

Entrepreneurial Women Share How To Crush Mediocrity
& Maximize Your Potential

Visionary Author
Dr. Sanja Rickette Stinson

DISRUPTING THE STATUS QUO

ISBN: 9798426411470

CONTENTS

DISRUPTING THE STATUS QUO

WE BELIEVED AND WE DID IT
Author Support Page

The visionary author and co-authors are sincerely thankful for the support of the following individuals who believed in us even before this book was printed. We feel blessed because of your support.

"I've learned that people will forget what you said, people will forget what you did, but people will never forget how you made them feel."
– Poet Maya Angelou

Marie Thibault
Darcy and Manami Thibault
Mark and Alynn Almeida
Aidyn Almeida
Harrison Almeida
Avalon Almeida
Marina (Tim) Thibault
Kirsten and Craig Munroe
Celine Thibault
Rae Ann Thibault
Renee Thibault
Dan and Shelia Thibault
Brendan Thibault
Jalaine Thibault
Shirley Thibault
Courtney Shea
Brooklyn Bye
Carter Bye
Marilyn Jones
Trudy Laucher
Pam Shaheen
Julie Stobbart
Carola Lorber-Grim
Marcia Wickenheiser
Tone Gulbaek-Pearce

Allison Faye
Rob and Bev Degleau
Denise Vanderwolf
Heather Cote
Karen (Lang) Brown
Pat Stewart
Melanie Hennig
Jean Fischer
Tina Toby
Morgan and Debbie Phillips
Allison Barlow
Rita MacKenzie
Stephanie Eisenbraun
Phoenix VanDyke
Shannon Smiley
Rhonda Smiley
Sophia Hodgins
RayAnna St. Amond
Rory Lambert
Darren Firloette
Ria Kaal
Francesca Anastasi
Phil Dutton
Maisie Dunbar
Zan Ray

Cheryl Campbell
Dan Varley
Brad Varley
Sandy Roberts
Joann Krajewski
Dale Vanbuskirk
Carolyn Saulstrom
Lucius Craig
Al Davie
Chris Elder
Josh Miller
Perfecto Brown
Thaddeus G. Buggs
Thor J. Buggs
Melbert L. Buggd
Shawn G. Buggs
Donald A. Buggs
Ronald E. Buggs
Shannette D. Buggs
Charde' Barnett
James Buggs
Shakiyah Buggs
Leroy & Janicca Covington
Ramona L. Buggs
Kryshaun D. Buggs
Robin C. Buggs
Atlantis Buggs
Lady Juanita Murchison
Prophetess LaTyrrell Pettitt
Leshele Silas-Armour
Jabar Lavelle Wheatley Jr
Serenity Barren
Patience Wheatley
Kristian Wheatley
Connor Stienmetz
Felicity Wheatley
Stan he Needham
Sherry Barren
Sammie Shelton

Kerria Snow
Shermaine Robinson
Katrina White
Toccara Steele
Terrence Hazzard
Dr. Nyree C. Tucker
Keyosha Ametchi
Joella Weaver
Jabar Wheatley Sr
Chief Dr. Quinton Tamba Taylor
de' Alexander
Wilferd Houston Jr.
Shanta Evans
Charles Weaver
Robert Weaver
Sylvia Shamyer
Libra Scuefield
Carlton Bowen
Kiara Jones Burgess
Sonji Hawkins
Valdeno Pinnock
Ross & Kiara Hall
Jeffrey & Tawana Hall
Nikisha Grinstead
Mary Streater Wyatt
Charles Rogers
Elaine Watkins
Sharmien Watkins
Zonia Ray
Virilyaih Scroggins
Patrice Yarbrough
Estrella Kenoly-Ramirez
Melvin Gilliam
Alnetta Morris
Kelby Farley
Rodria Watkins-Golden
Jamal West
Lisa Valdez
Louis Moorer

DISRUPTING THE STATUS QUO

Ronica Watkins-Babers
Charles Johnson
Tracy White-Davidson
Cara Rogers
Carrington Rogers
Kim J. Bright
Malik Melodies Sisterhood, Inc.
Maritza Arroyo
Kathleen D. Taylor
Randi Crawford
Sarina Jain
LaVada Humphrey
Cindy Lilavois Vazquez
Cathleen Lilavois
Mark Shambry
Henrietta Vines
Amanda Toles
Willie Akins
Nedra Joiner-Cole
Litanya Matlock-Brown
Annette Barker
Yara Buchanan
DeSandra Vaughn
Stephanie Humphrey
Tavia Jordan
Sebrina Brown
Kim Miller
Andrea Senior
Carshina Washington
Pamela J. Lawrence
Toi L. Salter
Kimyada M. Wellington
Karen Tribble
Michael Tribble
Beverly Childress
TSheeka Gibbs
Kimberly Haynes
April Carter
Lajuantonette (Wanda) Wade

Wanette Vines
Jeremy Vines
Angie Vines
Travis Vines
Dr. Lorri Cobbins
Carla Johnson
Dana Bryant
Rose Rivera
Terri & Calvin Higgins
Cathy & Robert Dale
Laura Worlds
Norma J. Mapp
Maurice Green
Tony Powell
Yasmin Curtis
Veronica Ford
Pattie Cuevas
James A Roberts
Lyman Harvey
Marcus C Evans
Angie Middleton
Tracey Slaughter Hardick
Cydyna Lee
Shirley McInnis
Lekeisha Hawkins
Sarah Roberson
Satoya Russell
Margo A Bel,l M.D.
Keshuna Franklin
Jessica Turner
Ramona Burress, PharmD
Robin Pettit
Carol Ann Pettit
Renee Linton
Linda M Davis
LiYana Baker
Eugenia Butler
Carmen Sanchez
Priscilla Price

DISRUPTING THE STATUS QUO

Pattie Guinn
Caitlin Snyder
Dr. Maria Crawford
Neesha Stringfellow
Shanna Nea
Rachel Jones
Tonica Boyd
Misty Boyd
Kim McClinton
Dr. Nona Parker
Dr. Glenda McCullum
Kara May
Lisa Daniels
Traci Brooks
Juliana Onalaja
Revita Prowell
Kisha Causey
Eugenia Olison
Mary Allen
Debbie Griggs-Holiday
Joyce Randall
Josie Allen
Paula Sledge
Shuntella Richardson
Kentrica Coleman
Paulette Ford
Kaaron Whiteside
Luwana Johnson
Nicole Holmes
LaSharne Johnson
Myra Penny
Tiffany Sledge
Roy Rolling
Helen Banks
Michele Evans-Brock
Cynthia Anglin
Lisa Dixon
Hattlyne Leonard
Yvonne Henry

Nancy Milsap-Thompson
Wanda Hope
Lori Bowden
Bria Bowden
Lacie Allen
Shauna Battle
Frances Cunningham
Fayrene Johnson Muhammad
Osei David Andrews-Hutchinson
Thomas Reeves
Crystal Reeves
Lacie Reeves
Jamar Allen
Jovon Allen
Janet Hill
Eddie & Debra Taylor
Larry Morrissette
Janessa Drayton
David Esposito
Ora Frierson
Morsie Williams
Wardell & Felicia Lindsey
Meri Bacon
Lilanga Dhanapala
Tidimogo Gaamangwe
Melody Byrd
Jasmine Singleton
Tiffany Sledge
Bishop William A Spann
Erikka Gordon
Shirri Buchanan
April Cosper
Lena Wilkerson
Britney Crank
Tory Moore
Eric McMullan
Maurice Riddle
Charita Jeffery
Darryl Lewis Jr.

DISRUPTING THE STATUS QUO

Terrance Jeffery
Cassandra J Witherspoon
Leslie M. Witherspoon
Precious Mays Matthews
Sherron Strong
Taneka Dixon- Robinson
Brian McCrae
Michael Thompson
Kaaron Whiteside
Bertha Moore
Irma Spencer
Donna Davis-Williams
Taniya and Floyd Jones
Apostle Jeremiah Fleming
Ronald Britton
Pastor Ellie Moss
Dr. Jasmine Zapata
Lilada Gee
Joe and Tena Brown
Taria Holman
Roxy Trent
Kathy McClure
Nina Jackson
Quincy Trent
Dr. Nancie Murphy & Pastor
Martyce Murphy
Pastor Dollie & Mr. Buster
Sherman
David and Sandra Reynolds
Melvin and Lori Terry
Brittney Britton
Juliet Cooper-Allen
Sherrie Jones
Charlestine Joyner Hudson
John and Sherry Lucille
Rev. Dr. Alexander and Jackie Gee
Pastor Pat Turner
Mickey and Debra Reynolds
Barry and Jerene Tucker

Constance Roby
Brenda L. Miles
Deirdre Suggs
Melissa Seamon-Johnson
Gregory Kidd Sr.
Barbara Ross-Lawrence
Joseph Love
Dilenia Garcia-Love
Tatiana Johnson
Dian Hoover
Essie Pough-Pope
Bridgett Curry-Allen
Wanda & Raymond Patrick
Vicki Carter-Street
Amy Aurelio
Sabrina Drummer
Michael & Julianne Baker
Voneita Whitehead
Michele Mickey Brown
Patrice Cowan
Billie Robinson
Apostle Deborah Campbell-
Smith
Ruby Warnell
Kenyatta Boone
Julian Scott
Vornada Snyder
Dorothy La Bon-Jackson
Stephaine Gordon
Debra Ali
Karen Johnson
Vivian Cook
Verlena Peters
La Rina Lewis
Leon Bowens
Curley Lumpkin
Jacqueline Anderson
Kendra Cowan
Vanessa Robinson

DISRUPTING THE STATUS QUO

Theresa & Frank Cowan III
La Toya D Smith
Tekeesha Cowan
Rachel Thomas
Paulette & Art Tiggs
Carla Hill
Kristen McGrew-Smith
Cynthia Corona
Frank Cowan IV
Annette M Alexander
Deanna Roberson
Afrl Alelani
Ramonalisa Parham
Renee Linton
Jamie Clay
Merle Robinson
Michelle Curtis
Litanya Matlock Brown
Evtrece Matlock
Patricia Matlock
Letrusia May
Coach Mike
Kela Jones
Shawnie Jones
Kimberly Brown
Terria Epting
Tracey Otis Mosley
Elizabeth Otis
Annette Meek
Janet Lunn
Shirley Fields
Cerita Brown
Stephanie Morgan Harris
Neka Curtis
Eula Latrice Boyce
Quentin Holloman
Charmaine "Cha Cha" Rickette
Marseil Jackson
Theartis Camara

Dee Hughey
Momma "D" Lewis University
Marcella Holley
Sonsaray Rickette
Pastor Barbara Brown
Lucy Redmond
Rochelle Simpson
Charlotte Myers
Ashley Moore
Markeyia Smith
Brianna Wright
Jewel Simpson
Fanniet Means
Judy Brooks
Alyssa Rhone
Tia Whitley
Avis LaVelle
Cynthia Val-Chapman
Donna Smith-Bellinger
Cheryl Grace
Carol Adams, PhD
Nelvia Brady, PhD
Sylvia Hope Daniels
Kim Lee
Sheila Townsend
Taffy Howard
Tanya Ball
Beverly Lumpkin
Debra Wesley
Margaret Garner
Marion Shuck
Pam Smith

INTRODUCTION

By Dr. Sanja Rickette Stinson
Visionary Author of Disrupting the Status Quo
3X Author | Nonprofit Founding CEO
Empowerment Speaker | Business Coach

As far back as biblical times, there have been many "disruptors" who arose to meet the seemingly insurmountable challenges they faced. Notable biblical examples of these strong women include the five daughters of Zelophehad; Deborah the judge; Esther; and Mary, the mother of Jesus, among many others.

And today, in the 21st century, we don't have to look far to find women who are disrupting the status quo and who have crushed mediocrity: Harriet Tubman, a woman of courage and vision; Carol Moseley Braun, the first African-American congresswoman; Michelle Obama, the first black first lady of the United States; Kamala Harris, the first female and first African-American vice president. There are countless others who have succeeded in disrupting the status quo and crushing mediocrity.

My vision for this book came after pondering the differences and similarities between an entrepreneur woman and person and an entrepreneurial woman and person. Here's how to distinguish between the two.

An entrepreneur is an individual who designs and launches a new business, often a small business. And entrepreneurial individuals are those with skills that enable them to identify and make the most of every opportunity and learn from their setbacks and failures. They possess skills that propel them to soar and be successful in various settings. Entrepreneurial mindsets are often focused on completing multiple projects.

I can now see how I've constantly challenged and disrupted the status quo in my own life. At a young age, I owned an

1

insurance brokerage firm. This was in the early 1990s, and it was one of my first attempts at becoming an entrepreneur. I secured several large and significant insurance companies, namely Hartford and Travelers Insurance.

In addition, I worked on the frontline in the fight against redlining. Redlining was the practice of arbitrarily denying or limiting financial services and insurance to specific neighborhoods, generally because their residents were people of color. I remember being fearless, resilient, and willing to challenge anything to bring about change for my family and community. This entrepreneurial venture failed. Even though I had accomplished something others around me hadn't, I still felt like a failure. I had settled for a life centered on mediocrity, allowing my past to define my future. Mediocrity is everywhere, and it can snowball and happen to the best of us, including you!

It took me a while to regain my footing, but there was a turning point when I started believing in myself again, believing that I was enough, that I could be not only an entrepreneur but also a successful one. I decided to rise above my failures because I was created to win!

I encourage you to dive deep into the stories shared in *Disrupting the Status Quo*. This book is about everyday women who step out in faith and challenge every aspect of their purpose with a zeal to disrupt the status quo and crush the mediocrity that held them back. The stories within this book are written by ordinary women, including a business owner, nonprofit executive, ministers, coaches, a trainer, teachers, mothers, grandmothers, and great-grandmothers.

Their decision to be driven by their entrepreneurial quest and move beyond their comfort zone has propelled them to become authorpreneurs, challenging and disputing the status quo while consistently crushing mediocrity.

Join me in celebrating each of the elite co-authors of *Disrupting the Status Quo,* Kearn Cherry and Dorothy P. Wilson. They have crushed mediocrity and decided to selflessly share the stories that will preserve their legacies.

I hope that these stories will convince you that you can also crush mediocrity and start living an undefeated life, that you can disrupt the status quo by walking with a new mindset and a new conviction that you are worth it! Now get to crushing!

DISRUPTING THE STATUS QUO

CHAPTER 1

Permission to SOAR
Transform Your Purpose
— Crush Mediocrity

"Don't allow mediocrity to blindside your visions."

Dr. Sanja Rickette Stinson

I'm Dr. Sanja Rickette Stinson. I live in Chicago, often called the Windy City. As an entrepreneurial woman who is continually crushing mediocrity, I will share my story.

During my childhood, I faced many ups and downs. I was challenged by the setbacks of being a little girl of color who came from a large family that lived below the poverty line, and I suffered from a severe and noticeable speech impediment that resulted in my failing several grades in elementary school. The struggle continued throughout high school, college, and beyond. My teachers told me that I wasn't good enough to consider seeking a higher education. But this gave me the impetus to give myself *Permission to SOAR*. Later, I was repeatedly told that the highest level of education I could earn would be a certificate. After completing three and a half years of doctoral courses, I once again defied all obstacles and gave myself *Permission to SOAR*.

Constant thoughts of failure, believing I needed to belong to different groups, and seeking acceptance in all the wrong places continued into my adulthood. I was anguished with thoughts of always wanting to belong to something I was not welcome to be a part of, or I was being used just for the resources I could bring. I was never recognized for the talented or innovative visionary that I was. These inadequacies led me to want to prove that I was worthy. I ended up getting mired in mediocrity because I didn't want to be known as a failure; I didn't want others to see that I had failed at several things, nor did I ever want to be seen as one who had been defeated.

Constantly seeking validation from others started to erode the God-given visions within me, allowing me to sink deeper into mediocrity and prompting me to exhibit the behavior that comes with such negativity. The reality is that I failed miserably at several entrepreneurial ventures, but I didn't quit!

From the time I was a child, I witnessed the power of being an entrepreneur. I knew what it looked like, how it felt, the accomplishment and freedom it brought. However, not everyone does. Some people never move beyond believing that the safest path is to get a job or build a career and prepare for retirement. And for some, that might be great. If you are reading this book, you are ready to crush mediocrity by giving yourself *Permission to SOAR*. Don't expect considerable support from family at first, but they often will come around. Close friends might not grasp your vision and might shy away from supporting you. Some will also eventually come around.

The first reality check is recognizing that mediocrity exists at some point in everyone's life. Whether playing it safe began in your childhood or started during your adult years, you must give yourself *Permission to SOAR*. By walking in your purpose, you can break every chain that keeps you anchored to mediocrity. There is always a temptation to accept an average life, which is the path to never living beyond mediocrity. Who knows whether you might be the one chosen by God to break the chain of mediocrity within your family's lineage?

One of my favorite biblical stories that relates to crushing mediocrity and shifting one's family lineage is found in the book of Numbers, chapters 13-14. The scripture tells about 12 men who were sent out to scout the Promised Land for the godchildren who had left the bondage of Egypt.

The Bible says that all returned many days later. They reported having seen giants in the land, and many of the men were panicked, ready to accept living an average life because of fear. Yet, two of the men, Caleb and Joshua, disagreed, believing that the people were well equipped to take the land. The two had both vision and determination to soar above. They were defying the majority and not giving in to doubt or obstacles. The two focused on what could be accomplished by faith and not by sight. They presented solutions. They were not fazed by the size of the giants but were impressed by the size of their God. With a bulldog's determination and vision to possess the land, Caleb and Joshua gave all *Permission to SOAR* and to face the fear of the unknown, to be willing to crush mediocrity and fulfill the promise of taking the land and walking in their purpose. They did not allow mediocrity to blindside the vision that would have kept them from transforming the lives of all.

At the root of mediocrity is the craving to be safe and secure, resulting in remaining average. One of my favorite sayings is that "Average will not be a part of my legacy." If you are going to preserve and create a legacy, you must be willing to give up the safety net.

Refusing to fail is another tie that binds us to mediocrity. Permitting yourself to fail is a perquisite of crushing mediocrity. Be determined to dream again and again and again. I did! Several of my businesses failed, and while I wanted to wallow and quit, quitting was not an option, just as accepting a life of mediocrity should not be an option.

The temptation to accept mediocrity is always around. It is safe; it is comfortable; it is what some expect you to accept. It's up to you and you alone to give yourself *Permission to SOAR*. It took me a while to give myself *Permission to SOAR* and *grow*. It meant I had to stop looking for acceptance from the majority, accept that I was among the minority, and be all right with that.

My breaking moment happened in June 2009. That is when I decided to give myself *Permission to SOAR*, which transformed my purpose. I started on the journey to crush and break every chain of mediocrity and take control of my destiny. I had heard too often that I was old; my time had passed; no one was going to take me seriously, but I would no longer allow what others said to affect me.

Here are a few steps I've taken as an entrepreneurial woman to crush mediocrity, and now I have given myself *Permission to SOAR!*

First, **Embrace Being Vulnerable**: We learn in childhood to defend ourselves in many ways, but this can hurt us as we reach adulthood. When you give yourself *Permission to SOAR*, be willing to be vulnerable by embracing your flaws, your mess ups, and the many cracks that come from being human, and allow others to see it.

Second, **Crushing Mediocrity Is Not Connected to Age**: Age is just a number and has nothing to do with walking in your purpose. So, give yourself *Permission to SOAR* with a determination to do it!

Third, **Invest in Your Visions and Dreams**: It took me many years to break the cycle of mediocrity when it came to investing in my visions and dreams. Breaking mediocrity will cost you; it doesn't come free. If you aren't willing to invest in you, how can you expect others to?

Fourth: **Be a Part of the Minority, and Not the Majority**: When you give yourself *Permission to SOAR*, don't expect everyone to jump on the bandwagon with you, or you will be disappointed. Even as other voices might be louder than yours, let go of the safety net called validation from others and start crushing mediocrity. Give yourself *Permission to SOAR* and go!

Fifth, **Remain Coachable**: Being coachable has everything to do with your attitude and not your skills. Your attitude sets the tone for success; your skills are what will get you there. A coachable individual is willing to grow, recognizing that there is always room for improvement. A person who is unwilling to accept coaching is a person who is content to live a life of mediocrity.

Today is the day to give your *Permission to SOAR* and *Crush Mediocrity*.

DR. SANJA RICKETTE STINSON

Dr. Sanja Rickette Stinson is the founder and CEO of Matthew House, Inc., which provides daytime services to homeless citizens. In its thirty years of existence under Dr. Stinson's leadership, the organization has grown from delivering essential services to providing seventy-three units of permanent supportive housing. Dr. Stinson stresses that homelessness is an experience that people go through, not a label that defines who they are.

In addition to serving as the founding CEO of Matthew House, Dr. Stinson is an author, cleric, and entrepreneur. She holds roots in a generational legacy of entrepreneurship and ministry, having been raised by her entrepreneurial parents, Gus and Mary Rickette, who founded Uncle Remus Saucy Chicken on Chicago's west side.

Dr. Sanja grew up with a profound respect for business and humanity, and these ethics translated into a strong advocacy for the merger of marketplace and ministry -- values she reveres as priceless. She is the founder of Dr. Sanja's Coaching & Consulting, which assists both profit and nonprofit businesses, and she specializes in helping entrepreneurial women over the age of forty to build the confidence to propel lasting legacies. She is also the founder of Women on the Frontline International Fellowship, which helps women find and walk in their purpose. She is an ordained minister serving as the apostolic covering for various ministries and churches.

Dr. Stinson the founding pastor of Victory & Grace Christian Church Chicago and serves as the apostolic covering for True Love Christian Church-Chicago while overseeing two churches: one in Ghana, West Africa; and other in Grand Rapids, Michigan. After spending six impactful years as the host of the weekly internet television program, "Women on the Frontline," Dr. Stinson in 2019 founded, as part of the BGK Network, the Ruach Covenant Channel, creating a platform to assist micro-ministries in spreading the Word of God through media, using innovative and state-of-the-art technology. She has authored two books, Hidden Impact, a collaborative project with the Women on the Frontline, released in 2018; and Vision Unleashed ~ Legacy Ignited, released in March 2020. Dr. Stinson is also a number-one best-selling author of the book, Possibilities Unlimited, an anthology project with the legendary Les Brown and international speaker, Dr. Cheryl Wood.

Dr. Stinson earned her bachelor's degree from DePaul University, a Master of Divinity degree from McCormick Theological Seminary, a Master of Education from Concordia University, and a Doctor of Ministry from Northern Theological Seminary.

Influenced by the belief of purpose being birthed in the lives of others, Dr. Stinson shows no signs of stopping. When she is not out exhorting the world to live out their life's vision, she is an asset to her communal body and a loving member of her family and friendship circles.

Dr. Sanja Rickette Stinson: Business Coach, Serial Entrepreneur Coach, Mentor, Leader, Trailblazer. Humanitarian, Minister.
Visionary Author of Disrupting the Status Quo
WEBSITE: www.drsanja.com
EMAIL: sanja@drsanja.com
SOCIAL MEDIA: @dr.sanjarickette

CHAPTER 2

WHY NOT!

BY DOROTHY P. WILSON
Elite Co-author

The proof, the power, of being a "disruptor" is not only seen in those amazing, winning moments, captured in photos posted on Facebook and Instagram.

No, it also can be seen in the failures, the lowest points in life, when even friends cautiously glance at you with eyes that say, "I told you so."

You will never become a real disruptor, one who challenges the status quo, until you're willing to risk falling, risk losing it all. A real disruptor is not defined by losses. She is defined by her willingness to take her own path, draw her own course, to be different — despite the odds, despite what and how others are doing.

The step from mediocrity over into disruption often is forged from pain, resistance, challenges, tears — and a searing determination to thrive and break out no matter what.

We tend to look at the ones who have become disruptors with admiration, and we should, because for every single disruptor, there are a thousand others who have become comfortable in the seat of "Just Enough." It's easy to run with the pack; it's another thing altogether to break forth and tear a new path.

That tear will cost you everything. But the rewards may give you more than you ever dreamed of …

As I look back now, at age 60, it has become easier and easier for me to say, "Go big — or go home. Why bother doing it if you're not going to play big? This type of thinking, this attitude, is a hallmark of the disruptor. She is looking straight at the finish line. She's looking past the obstacles. She is willing to eat fear for breakfast. Every day.

"What if I step out there and fall flat on my face?" Well, I say,

"What if you step out there and find that you have a greatness within you that you never knew you had?" Ha! Do it afraid.

I can recall so many times when I wanted to be stopped by "What if…" Those nagging negative thoughts were debilitating, compressing me into a small corner. But then I would think back to my momma, nicknamed Essie, who never fully realized all of her aspirations. And then I would lift my eyes with a fierce determination, and in my heart, I would say, "I am who God says I am. I have greatness within me!"

Yes, I have faced many, many situations that should have caused me to want to shrink back into a smaller place, a comfortable space. In those times, the choice was clear to me: Stagnate or disrupt.

I chose to become a disruptor when I, led by God, took a book project featuring 32 authors and catapulted it into an international faith conference and podcast/show seen and heard in 20 countries. Who says the goal of a book project is to just produce a book? It can be a seed that thrusts forth into an international movement. Why not!

I chose to become a disruptor when Kearn Cherry and I determined to birth Success Women's Conference in 2015. We had been sitting around yapping for some time, saying "Somebody should create a women's conference that … ." We stopped talking and started creating. Why not!

I chose to become a disruptor when I was laid off from my newspaper career after 28 years in 2012. Every fear inside me screamed, "Take the easy route. You can apply and get just about any corporate job you want here on the Coast." Well, I said, "Nah. I'm never going to give someone else that level of control over me again." I went from asking my boss in November 2011 what else I needed to do, training wise, to become a publisher, to purchasing a large share in a magazine three months later and giving myself the title of publisher. Compete for advertising dollars from my former employer? Why not!

I chose to become a disruptor in 1984 as a fresh college graduate when I decided that my job title of reporter didn't define me. I stepped forward and began to learn every job in that newsroom. I didn't have to ask for a promotion. I was already doing the job at the next level when the slot opened. I positioned myself to write my own job description. Why not!

I chose to become a disruptor in 1980 when Momma and big sis, Carolyn, said, "You better not go off to that big university. That's a white school, and we don't have money to be sending you every month." Well, I entered the University of Georgia, and despite being the youngest of six children, became the first to graduate from college. Why not!

Yes, that's right. Why not! Why not YOU? It's time to break out of the ordinary. You have greatness within you. But no one will ever know it if you're not willing to break through. Say, why not!

DOROTHY P. WILSON

Dorothy P. Wilson is an award-winning publisher and editor who creates platforms to help amplify messages and elevate brands. She does that through publishing books, developing magazines, and developing creative marketing strategies.

She offers 30-plus years of experience of wisdom in the publishing and marketing fields; and owns multiple successful businesses, including Gulf Coast Woman, DWilson & Associates, CWR Digital Gulf Coast, and Mighty Men Movers MS.

She is host and founder of FaithInspiration Network and Living Faith Out Loud Conference. People in 20 countries watch and listen to the FaithInspiration Network.

She is co-founder of a top-10 conference for professional women, Success Women's Conference, reaching 20,000-plus in 2021.

Her success reaches across multiple platforms and levels, and she has been recognized broadly, including as a Top 10 Woman Business Owner by the National Association of Women Business Owners (NAWBO); SBA Women in Business Champion; one of the Top Most Influential African-Americans in the State of Mississippi; Humanitarian of the Year; Magazine Publisher of the Year for Mississippi.

She has helped dozens of clients produce best-selling books. Her personal book projects include New York Times bestseller "Katrina: 8 Hours That Changed the Mississippi Gulf Coast Forever," "Little Book of Weapons: How To Defeat Your Giants," and Amazon-bestsellers "Unboxed: 25 Women Share How To Break Free & Soar" and "Live Your Faith Out Loud."

www.dwilsonandassociates.com
FACEBOOK & INSTAGRAM: @thatmediaqueen

CHAPTER 3

YOU DON'T FIT THE CULTURE

BY KEARN CHERRY
Elite Co-author

As a young person, I never felt like I fit in. I was different in so many ways. My name was definitely different and unique — Kearn. I was raised as a Jehovah Witness so we didn't celebrate holidays and all the birthdays. No Pledge of Allegiance and all those things that other kids just did because they were told to. I was definitely one of the quiet wallflower types and probably was classified as a nerd. I was competitive on the academic level, but as far as what the popular kids participated in, that was absolutely NO!

Of course, everyone thought they knew what to expect from me. I was going to finish at the top of my class with my brother and off to a big college. Well, that did not happen. I crossed the stage at my high school graduation seven months pregnant. I could have fallen apart and just got a job, but that would not be me. I started college when my son was three weeks old and started working on the military base as a medical secretary. I was determined that I would finish school like all of my siblings. Having a child as a teenage mom was definitely unexpected, but it was not going to determine my life journey.

In some situations, challenges like this can change a person's life for the worse. I decided that my current situation would not determine my destiny. I knew that I could accomplish anything, therefore it only fueled my success. After getting married to my son's dad, we traveled with the military. We spent time overseas in a mostly remote area and then in Arizona, another remote area. I noticed many of the military wives would stay at home or return to their family. Being in a remote location really can get lonely, so I decided to adapt. I believed in family being together.

Returning to our hometown and starting a business would seem like the ideal situation. My husband and I are both from the Mississippi Gulf Coast. So when we finally started our business, it seemed like it would be a breeze. That was not the case. We worked hard to be involved in our local community. I joined nonprofit boards, chamber of commerce boards, and other women organizations because we truly believe that as business owners you have a responsibility to your community. Giving back with your time and money is a must. Naturally, I thought we were making deep connections in our community. I was president, vice president or fundraiser chair for several boards, always willing to step up and do things that others did not want to do. After applying for a board position that in my mind I would fit perfectly and make great contributions, I was informed that I didn't fit the culture. I found that interesting and frustrating at the same time, especially since I had known the person who said it for years. I was even told by another person that if I just changed up my look and how I approach things, that would help me the next time. Well, I am not your "cookie cutter" board member, so I decided it was time to make my own impact in the community. I created conferences that served needs like my caregivers' conference. I also teamed up with my pastor's wife and produced a conference for Christian women. I focused on expanding my brand by leading other women's organizations and other chambers.

I decided that no one would stifle my ability to impact the community or create powerful connections. I formed collaborations with people who were interested in me being a part of the board, events and so on. I took my talents and gifts where they would be appreciated and utilized for the good of the community. I realized that it was in my power to change the "status quo" and open the door to opportunities for others. Basically, if others thought I was not good enough, I would create my own opportunities. Sometimes you have to become the champion for others. This can appear in different ways, but it is up to us to change how things operate.

As a community leader, I decided that it was time to do things differently. While leading organizations and creating for the community, the things I did would look different. Instead of operating in "status quo" I decided to run things differently. Most local organizations are typically autocratic, especially when choosing who will be a part of the decision-making. By allowing others to be involved in the decision-making process, people feel more included. My goal is to create a collaborative environment that allows everyone to excel.

In order to see change in your community, organization, or in life, you have to be willing to take risks, step out in faith and do something different. I believe that everyone can WIN, but sometimes you have to create some disruption in order to make that happen. Whatever you do, don't let someone else's "status quo" keep you from accomplishing what God has called you to do.

In the end, I realized that I was called to create my own culture and help others reach their success!

Being a disruptor can be extremely rewarding.

KEARN CHERRY

Speaker, 16X #1 best-selling author, and award-winning busi-

nesswoman, Kearn Crockett Cherry is a tycoon with a "leg-up" in successful entrepreneurship. Laying to rest any stigma surrounding the stagnancy of female leadership in the Deep South, Kearn has enjoyed more than two decades of excellence, as co-owner of PRN Home Care. She is often called the "Butts in the Seats Queen".

The Success Women's Conference is an award winning-business leadership conference attracting an annual audience of over 17,000 attendees worldwide. Kearn Cherry and her partners have a reputation for revolutionizing the way women interpret both public speaking and business, on a global scale. Kearn also has facilitated two virtual conferences; "Level Up Summit" and "Power Up Summit".

In 2001, Kearn Cherry effortlessly graced the pages of one of the most popular publications in the world, Essence Magazine. Kearn was recognized as the "Comeback Queen", confirming her commitment to exemplify dynamic business agility. Today, Kearn is a familiar face on several magazine covers. Recently featured on Black Enterprise, VIP Magazine, Speakers Magazine, Sheen Magazine, and her very own, are amongst her favorites.

Giving birth to Amazon #1 best-selling book, "Trailblazers Who Lead: Unsung Heroes", comprising 29 stories featuring several well-respected female entrepreneurs, moguls, and business professionals.

Kearn remains diligent in helping entrepreneurs reach their destined potential. She recently released #1 bestseller - "Make It Happen" anthology with 30 authors. She is the visionary for "Trailblazers Who Lead II" and her new anthology, "Undefeated", features 100 women sharing secrets to winning.

http://www.kearncherry.com
kearn@prnhomecareservices.com
SOCIAL MEDIA -@kearncherry or @kearncrockettcherry

CHAPTER 4

ARE YOU WHINING OR ARE YOU WINNING?

BY CHARMAINE V. RICKETTE

I never lose. I either win, or I learn! This quote gives me life. Being an entrepreneur has many peaks and valleys, and I've experienced both. When you think of a valley experience, you think of doom, death, stagnation, disparity, and failure. It certainly is not a comfortable place to be in. The valley experience is an entrepreneur's testing and proving ground.

There are three types of entrepreneurs. Some entrepreneurs, like me, obtained their businesses through inheritance. I call this the generational or legacy entrepreneur.

Some leave their jobs to become their own boss. I call this the step-out-on-faith entrepreneur.

And some come out of the womb selling ice to an Eskimo. I call this the serial entrepreneur.

Regardless of which you are, you almost certainly can expect to have a valley experience. The moves you make, your mental preparedness, and tenacity will be tested and questioned by others and yourself during uncertain times. I've been in the valley more than I care to remember. Some of those times were of my own doing, and some were out of my control. I am by nature, and most importantly by faith, a positive thinker. I don't project a "woe-is-me" attitude when things are low. Instead, I intentionally turn my deep-valley experiences into mountaintop visions. Yes, I said it: Valleys are meant to be preparation times for a new vision!

When my parents appointed me to take over the family business, most people thought I had instant riches. I was excited; I had a big vision for the future. I wanted the restaurant to grow from being a neighborhood ma-and-pa business to a nationally beloved brand. I knew it would take hard work, diligence, and studying other brands I aspired to emulate. I knew there would be a lot of internal and external growing pains. I just didn't know that it would take so long. I certainly thought that after twenty years, I would be much further along. I thought we'd have a multitude of stores instead of just five. Some of my lowest points were the continual rejections I received when I was looking for financing to expand the restaurant. I have been turned down at least twelve times from traditional and non-traditional lenders. Always hearing "no" can wear most people down, cause self-doubt, and prompt some to give up. But I'm not most people. I always question lenders to see why they turned me down so that I can learn what I need to do to turn that no into a yes.

Although it is very disappointing to get turned down, especially when I can find no valid reason for rejection, I keep pursuing my vision for expansion, and I remind myself that many before me took longer than expected to reach their vision. The real Col. Sanders was an entrepreneur who didn't become a professional chef until he was forty, didn't sell the first Kentucky Fried Chicken franchise until he was sixty-two, and didn't become an icon until after he sold his company when he was seventy-five. I also have three reminders that keep me going when I'm having a valley experience:

1. God doesn't give vision without provision.
2. I remind myself that this too shall pass.
3. Tomorrow is never a day of the week. It's my "do-over day," also known as "brand-new mercies."

During my Bible study and meditation time, I've learned the significance of the number three: Jesus prayed three times in the Garden of Gethsemane before His arrest. He was placed on the cross the third hour of the day (9 a.m.) and died the 9th hour (3 p.m.). There were three hours of darkness that covered the land while Jesus suffered on the cross. Three also relates to the Resurrection. Christ was dead for three full days and three full nights before being resurrected. I give myself three minutes, three hours, and sometimes three days to wallow in my valley experience. I'll take a nap, watch mindless TV, read about other winners to draw inspiration from, or play spades on my phone to clear my mind. After that, it's time to re-focus, strategize, and re-energize, because whining is a mindset that has no place in my mind.

The legendary Coach Vince Lombardi said, "Winning isn't everything, but wanting to win is." When you say that out loud, it sounds like an oxymoron. What's so great and motivating about trying to win if the consolation prize is "winning isn't everything?" The mind is the most powerful part of the body. Our minds release so much energy to help us perform exceptionally well. All of us have this potential, but only a few of us utilize the skill. Definitely, strong genes play a significant role in developing our mind power, but we can train ourselves to develop strong minds and achieve the impossible. Wanting to win is the seed you plant in your mind that drives you to succeed.

Most leaders are their own competition. They are constantly looking for ways to improve and learn from their wins, setbacks, and losses. Mark Cuban is one of the most relatable and successful entrepreneurs of the 20th century. He stated, "It's not about money or connections — it's the willingness to outwork and out learn everyone... And if it fails, you learn from what happened and do a better job next time."

Oftentimes, when you win at something, there is an immediate celebration and a sigh of relief from all the hard work, blood, sweat and tears it took to get there. After that, you move on to the next challenge. It's imperative that you don't move so fast. Athletes watch hours of film footage to learn how to improve. Did you know that they're not just watching the games they lost but also studying the games they won? Learning from a loss is important, sometimes costly, and certainly, humbling. Learning from a win is valuable, priceless, and even more humbling.

As an entrepreneur and leader, I've certainly had some wins. Uncle Remus Saucy Fried Chicken became the first non-national and black-owned restaurant to ever operate inside a Walmart. Uncle Remus Saucy Fried Chicken has been featured in local print and digital media as well as on the Travel Channel, giving the brand worldwide exposure. Our proprietary trademarked, delicious, and beloved mild sauce is now bottled. There are currently four restaurants open and operating; we operate a state-of-the-art food truck, and we own five trademarks. I did not accomplish these wins alone. Just as the old proverb says, "It takes a village to raise a child," it takes a team to build an empire. You can't win with a "me-against-the-world" or an "it's-my-way-or-the-highway" mentally. True leaders know their strengths, but most importantly, they know their weaknesses. The administrative side of running a business is not my happy place; I love technology but am not at all tech savvy. I'm also impatient when I know that an idea is great, and I want to move immediately, regardless of finances, total roll-out preparedness, or infrastructure readiness. This is where building a team that sees your vision and is willing to roll up their sleeves and work alongside you to see that vision fulfilled is important. Keep in mind that like your vision, the team you need will not be built overnight. Be vigilant and diligent about protecting your brand from those who are along only for the ride. As a woman of faith, I am very sensitive to the Holy Spirit when I build my team. I have not been the most obedient when it was time to sever some business and personal relationships. Lastly, listen to your team. If you have empowered them to seek out ways to grow the brand, be willing to try others' ideas and solutions.

There is so much more in store as I build this billion-dollar brand. We will partner with a financial entity that sees the value of the Uncle Remus SFC legacy, and we will expand our footprint by opening more stores locally and nationally. Our beloved mild sauce will be nationally distributed, and we will fulfill our vision to be a lasting impact in all the communities we serve.

These declarations are what fuels me. My pastor preached a sermon many years ago that I often recall. He said a boxing match is twelve rounds, and when you get knocked down, you get a ten-count to get up and try again. Your journey as an entrepreneur is much like a boxing match. Sometimes you're knocked down, beaten up, and have visible scars from your fight to victory, but you're not knocked out. Continue to dream and build your vision. The champion in you is not a whiner, but a winner.

CHARMAINE V. RICKETTE

Charmaine V. Rickette is president and CEO of Uncle Remus Saucy Fried Chicken, which was founded by her parents, Gus and Mary Rickette, over 50 years ago. Charmaine is the youngest of their 12 children.

Charmaine has breathed new life into the concept of the local, family-owned restaurant, building a sustainable business through operating system updates, a strong leadership team, and a commitment to employee training and engagement.

Under her leadership, Uncle Remus Saucy Fried Chicken made history when it became the first non-national and black-owned restaurant to operate inside a Walmart.

Charmaine believes in rehabilitation and second chances and has worked with city, state, and civic organizations to help inmates and displaced people transition back into the workforce.

Former gang members, substance abusers, and homeless citizens are now a part of her management team.

A natural communicator, Charmaine graduated from Columbia College where she studied broadcast journalism and earned a Bachelor of Arts degree in Liberal Arts. From 1985 to 1989 Charmaine was employed in the special events office of Chicago's Mayor Harold Washington. Charmaine worked with tourism, protocol, and PR for festivals and dignitary visits.

Charmaine completed business courses at the Living Word Christian Center's Joseph Center Business School and attended Pal's Business Excellence Institute. Charmaine also develops and mentors business owners and entrepreneurs.

Charmaine is the chairperson for the Austin African American Business Networking Association (AAABNA).

Her honors include winning the Chicago Defender Women of Excellence Award, the Launa Thompson Phenomenal Woman Award, and she has earned numerous other local civic and community accolades.

WEBSITE: CHICKCHATWITHCHARMAINE.COM
FACEBOOK & INSTAGRAM: CHARMAINEVRICKETTE

CHAPTER 5

SPECIAL NEEDS PARENTS HAVE NEEDS, TOO

BY DEBRA VINES

I am Debra Vines, a widow and mother of two adult children. My younger son, Jason, has autism. During Jason's lifetime, I have experienced the joys and pains of finding myself while raising a son with low executive functioning autism. And now, I am one of my community's leading advocates for special needs families.

I was married to the perfect partner and had an amazing child. I had a great career with what seemed like unending ambition and drive. No serious worries, no setbacks. But then, I became pregnant again unexpectedly. To tell you the truth, I really didn't want this pregnancy or to start this journey all over again. The doctor told me the pregnancy was high risk, that the baby was at increased risk of health problems before, during, and after delivery.

Becoming pregnant this second time had snatched my ideal life right from under me. And the possibility of what was happening inside my womb was even more gut-wrenching. My husband and I both were petrified. At the time, I didn't know that having to raise a special needs child would present questions I had never fathomed and take me on a journey to find the answers I needed to survive as a mother, a partner, and a business owner.

My prior pregnancy was normal, and my son was born healthy and with no complications. I think my expectations of pregnancy and childbirth were, "I was healthy; therefore, my baby will be healthy."

I delivered Jason at twenty-four weeks. Researchers have found differences in the brains of babies born before twenty-seven weeks who were later diagnosed with autism. But medical professionals didn't know this in the '80s when Jason was born.

He weighed two pounds, two ounces. He remained in the hospital for three months. Meanwhile, I felt isolated at home, as postpartum anguish set in. Raising a special needs child honestly felt exhausting, and I felt like dying.

And Jason's challenges didn't end with his being a preemie. We noticed developmental issues in Jason around sixteen months. He wasn't walking, talking, or meeting other crucial developmental benchmarks. We went to various doctors, soliciting second, third, fourth opinions. Finally, Jason was diagnosed with autism at eighteen months. My husband and I were unsure what this would mean for our child or for us. The only thing we knew about autism was from the movie Rain Man. Was my child going to be a card-counting savant in Vegas, non-verbal, or all the above?

As Jason grew, so did his list of challenging behaviors. He had tantrums and random outbursts when in unfamiliar places or when his normalcy or routine was tampered with.

During Jason's early years, my husband worked a night shift, and my family lived far away, so I was left to care for our son virtually on my own. I sacrificed my career and personal life to navigate Jason's life as a growing boy with special needs. As a parent of a developmentally challenged child, I didn't get to have anything to myself. I didn't have my own time. I didn't have control. I felt alone, frustrated, and overwhelmed.

Between doctor visits, specialist appointments, endless researching, and other caregiving responsibilities, it's no wonder we run out of time or money to take care of ourselves as parents. We need answers, but we barely have energy to formulate the questions.

No matter where I turned, I didn't find the answers or the support I needed, especially in my under-resourced neighborhood. But I did find drugs. Through moments of weakness and lacking the ability to cope with what I couldn't control, I began to use cocaine.

My husband didn't have the answers, either. Time after time, I would ruin our family finances to feed my addiction, but he wouldn't give up on me. I'd always run back to drugs, thinking that they would numb the pain, the feeling of being overwhelmed, the burden of having so many questions and so few answers.

Now, don't get me wrong: I was both a functioning addict and a functioning mom. The need to take care of my family had never left my mind, but I was willing to do it only on my own terms... with drugs. Even so, I wanted answers, but resources remained limited. Once, I collected discarded computer parts and actually built a computer so I would have a way to research autism. I was desperate to get high, but even more desperate to learn about what Jason was experiencing as an autistic child. I searched and searched for information and my next high.

The irony continued as my life spiraled out of control. I began stealing to get drugs and landed in jail a few times. The guilt began to wear on me as much as the crack. What few friends I had left faded away. I lost faith. I remember wanting to know why God felt I was "strong enough" to handle a special needs child. I wondered if this was something I deserved.

It felt like the drugs restored my control until I couldn't control my addiction or my actions. And it became harder to help Jason when I couldn't help myself. I despised myself.

I remember the very last time I was arrested. I didn't care about the amount of time they wanted to give me. All I knew was that I was exhausted. I was tired of waking up and thinking about getting high and ending my day thinking the same. I wanted something different for myself and for my family. So, while in jail, I turned my life around.

Rehab was difficult. Looking at myself in the mirror was burdensome. But the thought of being a healthier me for my family motivated me. I realized I had to love myself in order to love and properly raise my children. I regarded this process like college and made sure I participated in every single group session, attended my individual sessions, and completed all treatment requirements. I wanted to be better, stronger. I even decided to stay an additional three months past my rehab release date to make sure I could permanently kick this addiction.

It wasn't until I witnessed Jason reach milestones in his development that I realized how much I had taken for granted. It was Jason's determination that taught me how to heal and strengthen myself. It was Jason's journey as a person with a disability that helped me re-embrace my ability. My patience was fallible. My endurance was flaky. Yet, here was Jason, taking on the world as a young adult: eager to make his own sandwich, take out the trash, and order his favorite milkshake.

Fast forward to today when Jason is a grown man, taller than I am and with dreams that are as wide as his beautiful eyes. I must be honest; I underestimated Jason just as I underestimated myself, not understanding the purpose and possibility of my being. You can value your mistakes just as you do your triumphs. It is when I embraced my worthiness as a person, as a mother, as a partner, that I began to heal enough to care for Jason and myself.

And I had an epiphany: I realized that so many moms of special needs children have little to no support in their community. It has resulted in so many of us hating ourselves, letting ourselves go, not wanting to face the realities of what we deemed an imperfect child.

Raising Jason has slowly revealed my life's mission: to provide to other parents of special needs children the answers that I so achingly searched for. I started The Answer, Inc. to create resources and provide support to parents so they won't have to suffer as I did. We have established groups that provide information about resources and create dialogue for discussion and support of people with special needs. We also offer family and peer events to empower people with disabilities to practice acceptable public behaviors and hone socialization skills.

As for me, time healed my wounds of emptiness and regret. As Jason reached his teenage years, I felt myself becoming healthier, and I became a better mother and woman for my community. Ironically enough, Jason's diagnosis is what changed my life.

Being the mother to a special needs child allowed me to take a journey to provide answers where there were none for me. Although there are still more questions than answers, I hope this ignites a conversation to help families like mine live enriched and happy lives.

Now that Jason is an adult, his milestones into manhood are beautiful to witness — and my milestones into womanhood are beautiful to experience. As a growing adult, I often watch Jason possess the same tenacity and strength that it took me to survive the addiction and to overcome the depression. Now, as the founder/CEO of The Answer Inc., I am able to transfer that same tenacity, that same strength, over to families who struggle with the challenges of having a special needs child.

There are solutions to finding yourself again as a mother of a special needs child. One, prioritize self-care. It is okay to get away and ask for support. You deserve alone time, time with your friends.

Two, give yourself grace. You are a human... and it is okay to have bad days and make mistakes as a parent. Don't turn to negative vices when you are frustrated. If you see yourself slipping, get help immediately.

And three, create your own social life and time to enjoy what you like, even for a few minutes or an hour. It is important that you find yourself and learn to enjoy the things that make you happy. Create a social life outside of being a parent; it's healthy. And the happiness that you create for yourself is the same happiness you will need to raise your special needs child.

DEBRA VINES

Debra Vines deeply understands the importance of advocacy, community involvement, and partnership. Her son Jason was diagnosed with autism when was eighteen months old.

In 2007, she founded The Answer, Inc., a nonprofit organization that helps parents and caregivers navigate the systems of social services and academic institutions by providing case management/referral services, recreation, and resources for families with individuals who have autism or other developmental disorders.

She also knows how important it is to sincerely give selflessly to promote and create change in the lives of people with autism and other disabilities. Her greatest accomplishment has been to watch the families she has helped reach milestones that they were told would be unobtainable.

- *Senator Kimberly Lightford Women Committee*
- *Erikson Institute, Fellow*
- *Bellwood Chamber of Commerce, Board Director*
- *Department of Defense (Autism), Peer Reviewer*
- *Co-Host of 1390am Brunch Bunch Show*
- *Treasurer Michael Frerichs Community Leader Award*
- *Chicago Defender Women of Excellence Award*
- *Alpha Kappa Alpha Sorority Community Leader Award*
- *Delta Sigma Theta Community Leader Award*

- *Hillside Commission Dr. Martin Luther King Dream Award*
- *AAABNA Community Service Award*

WEBSITE: www.theanswerinc.org
FACEBOOK & INSTAGRAM: @debravines
EMAIL: thedvinesexperience@gmail.com

DISRUPTING THE STATUS QUO

CHAPTER 6

CHOSEN FOR THE JOURNEY: OWNING THE WOMAN, THE WIFE, THE MOTHER

BY DEBORAH C. ANTHONY

My name is Deborah C. Anthony, and I am from Joliet, Ill. I am an entrepreneurial woman who has crushed mediocrity by embracing every aspect of my colorful journey as a woman, a wife, and a mother. For many centuries, women all over the world have asked, "Who am I? What on earth am I here for? Is my job just to be a woman who takes care of everyone else? Is my identity hidden in my role as a wife, being a help to my husband? Or am I just called to raise children all my life?" Admittedly, a woman's role has many facets, which I choose to call colorful. What I really want to say to women all over the world is to *own it!* Own every phase of your life — every trial, every encounter that is good, bad, or mediocre. Know that it's okay that you don't have it all figured out.

Life has questions for all of us; however, the questions that so many women ask are similar and continue to crop up as we go through various stages of our lives. We wonder if we are doing what we are really called to do; we wonder if we're making the right decisions. I have asked myself these questions so many times. Now I stand at the age of forty-five and say, "I own it all! All the good decisions, all the bad decisions, all of it! I own me — the woman." The many hats I wear have often caused me to question my worth and my value and to question what I have really been chosen to do. I want to say to you, as I have had to say to myself, you are chosen. You are chosen for the journey that you are on right now. No one else could overcome the obstacles you have faced the way you did. No one could build the life you have created the way you have. No one could birth the fantastic children you have birthed. God made you for this time, so stand tall in all its splendor and own it!

I want to share with you the difference between who I am and what I do. Most of us are defined by what we do and not by who we really are. We go by the titles we've been assigned rather than by God's original plan for us.

In 2009 I was fired from my corporate job, and that crushed me because I never thought I could be as successful as I had been at that job. When I came out of college, I was convinced that the only thing I was good at was working for someone else. I never believed in myself enough to own my own business, or to do as I do now, help others to transform their lives by helping people build businesses, write books, and build brands. It was not until I was pushed out of my company that I began to look within myself and began to see my full potential; I was able to see what God had created in me.

Who I am …

I am now a woman of God who has truly embraced all that comes with being me. I stand firmly centered in knowing that I have been redeemed. Although I can be very serious and comical, I have the capacity to be extremely focused with business. I am not afraid to look into the mirror and see all that comes with being me. I am a task master driven to succeed; yet, on the other hand, I am an exciting and loving person — that is who I am. I no longer choose to identify myself with my experiences, or the people on my journey…. I now make a conscious decision to be whole in me. I was created to be not to just become. I am constantly chasing after the One who created me, to become like Him.

I am the woman who owns what I look like, because it is all a part of who I am. As I continue in this season of maturation, I am encouraged to write and share the many places of change and healing in my life. Even as I am writing now, I am experiencing some residue of brokenness, but I am also honestly recognizing that in my perceived weakness, God is strong, and that is what truly matters. He is strong in me!

I thought I was very good at looking at the details; upon reflection I now see that God wants me to look a little closer at those areas that I have overlooked. Although I am now whole, I am grateful for those times in my life when I couldn't see God's imprint on my life, because they brought me to Him.

What I do...

I can truly say that this question used to be easier to answer. I could ramble about who I thought I was to anyone. Many roles come to mind; I am:

A woman of God

A mother of six children

A wife of twenty-one years

An entrepreneur/business owner

An author of four books

A builder of businesses, Brands, and books

All those powerful areas that I thought defined me really are not as important as who I am. I appreciate all that I can do, but it is not who I am.

I have discovered roles are temporal in the eyes of God and that time and chance happen to us all. That does not take away from the great responsibility that each of us has or the weight that comes with each. It is so important to ascertain a balance in our make-up because each part of us makes up what I do. I often take many deep breaths and ask the Lord, "How shall I do what I have to do?" One day, the light bulb came on, and I realized that I cannot do anything without God, not even the smallest thing.

So now what do I do? I sit waiting for instruction, asking the Father what His daily plan is for me. He has a plan and a will for my life, and all I must do is rest and do just what He says. I do what He has called me to do each day, and only that. I no longer run around creating things to do. I will not lean into my intellect or understanding; rather, I consciously seek Him for what His plan is for my life.

The quest for the woman, the wife, the mother, began with the question, "Who are you?" I pray that in your questioning you find yourself in whatever stage you are in, realizing that you will evolve; you will grow and certainly will be stretched. You will feel as though you are dying and beg to be rescued from yourself. Staying the course is so critical. You must understand, there is only one you. There is only one blueprint that God has designed for your life, and you must walk in your purpose and destiny and in His timing to fulfill the promises that are in your life.

What I thought was so tough was sitting right there in front of me. It took me so long to understand the love of God, and yet it was so simple that even a child could understand. What I realized was my view of love was faulty, imperfect compared to the love from my Father. Before my surrender to accepting me, all of me, I had a confused view of how to receive and give love.

Juxtaposition means to place (different things) side by side (as to compare them or contrast them or to create an interesting effect). Juxtapose unexpected combinations of colors, shapes, and ideas - J. F. T. Bugental

I learned to embrace this word — juxtaposition — as I began to own all that God was designing in my life, realizing that my journey was taking me on many different voyages that had many different colors. Through it all, God's idea for my life never changed, and I could trust Him, for "He who promised is faithful." I no longer must live in shame or in questioning His plan. I can stand tall and squeeze the joy out of life, never forgetting to grow and go.

As you embrace your life's journey and all that has come with it to bring you to this treasured place in God, know that our God does not waste one ounce of our defeats, victories, or transitions — He uses all of it to cause us to be colorful with all the beautiful bounty of hues that He created.

No matter what stage of life you find yourself in as the woman, the wife, or the mother, I need you to know you were born for the moment you are standing in right now. God took His time and handpicked you for the season you are in. When you find yourself in doubt or in question, slow down and breathe:

YOU are CHOSEN for The Journey to be … Colorful.

A few steps to help you embrace your journey:

- Look into the mirror and say, "I embrace all that I see, every part of me, this woman."
- Find daily positive affirmations.
- Forgive yourself and forgive those who caused you pain; refusing to will hinder your seeing the bright future ahead, for it clouds your vision.
- Find accountability people who are willing to be honest with you and sharpen you, so you can grow and become better.
- Take time to laugh at yourself and your journey; look at every day as a learning experience knowing you can only get better from here.
- Stay the course, and even when it gets hard, know that God picked you for this journey.

DEBORAH C. ANTHONY

Deborah Anthony is a business coach, literary coach, and four-time author. She has been an industry leader for more than twenty years.

For the past twenty years, Deborah has helped hundreds of businesses stand out in their industries. Her goal is simple: to ensure your message and methods connect with your customers. She has a customized approach to connecting with you through groups or individualized coaching, researching your needs through a series of in-depth interviews, and developing a comprehensive report with valuable recommendations for how to improve your outcomes using the latest branding tools and concepts.

Beyond the analytical component, Deborah works extensively to uncover the heart and essence of your dream, idea, and what you are most passionate about, because that is what makes your brand unique and special. Whether we are creating a revolutionary brand to redefine an entire category or repositioning an existing brand, Deborah specializes in helping brands focus on who they are and what their values are.

Deborah is a proud graduate of DeVry Institute of Technology where she obtained a Bachelor of Science in Business Operations. She then matriculated through St. Xavier School of Management, obtaining her MBA. Deborah's educational and corporate business backgrounds have prepared her for the unique challenge of corporate training.

WEBSITE: www.deborahcanthony.com
FACEBOOK & INSTAGRAM: @Deborahcanthony

CHAPTER 7

YOU DON'T HAVE TO BE SOUL-ED OUT TO SUCCEED

BY WYNONA REDMOND

My name is Wynona Redmond. I am the founder and president of Wyn-Win Communications, Inc., a Chicago-based public relations agency that places an emphasis on health, business, faith-based, and community engagement. I am an entrepreneurial woman who has learned that you can crush mediocrity and succeed by not being "souled out."

Here's how that learning came alive for me.

I was at a Congressional Black Caucus prayer breakfast when the decision I'd been weighing was confirmed. Bishop Noel Jones was speaking. He chided the audience for not using the talents God gave them. He exhorted us to get off our knees and stop writing speeches for our bosses and become our own boss. It was in that moment that I made the decision to become an entrepreneur, and Wyn-Win Communications was born. That was nine years ago.

To hear Bishop T.D. Jakes tell it at his Woman Thou Art Loosed retreat several months later, I was a chick who, having grown too large for its shell, had to peck its way out to grow. When you grow, you can't stay in the same place. You have to get out. That was where I found myself. Throughout my nearly three decades-long career as a communicator, I had devoted my talents to helping corporations and brands connect with the community through messaging and philanthropy. My work was never mediocre, but working for someone else had become mediocre. My calling demanded more from me than just making a living: I am hard-wired to make a difference.

We spend so much time at work that, according to Jesus CEO, it is holy ground. For me, making the leap to start my own company was the confirmation of the Parable of the Talents. Viewed through this lens, mediocrity could simply be burying my God-given talents and not multiplying them. Thus, my making the decision to be an entrepreneur, to determine the direction and use of my time and talents, crushed mediocrity. And that is when I truly understood that God is my source.

Commit your actions to the Lord, and your plans will succeed -Proverbs 16:3

Fast forward to today. The past two years have been an unprecedented time in our nation's history. A global pandemic. Persistent social and racial inequity. Hardening political polarization. Economic uncertainty and its impact on individuals and families. All this led me to an epiphany: we don't have that much time. We've really got to focus on building the community, building the infrastructure, building the relationships -- getting the word out. I want to use my time to say "what can we do to help promote and educate and advocate for a cure for cancer? What can we do to promote the safety of our communities and our kids?"

Choose ye this day whom you will serve. -Joshua 24:15

Although I have always been guided by my Christian values, I wanted there to be no disputing in 2022 and beyond that I am intentional about applying those same values to my business, so it is crystal clear to all. In 2021 I decided to say "no" to business that does not align with our core values. As an agency we made the transformational decision to work only with people and organizations we believe in and accept projects only if they make a difference. We decided to hire clients instead of being hired. My conscious decision and strategy were that for Wyn-Win to work with you, the benefit has to come back to the community.

Working for Good

Being selective and intentional about the work we accept means not being for sale or being "souled" out. So, we're not going to sell casinos; we're going to be a force for getting life and death messages out into the community with churches. We're not going to sell cannabis dispensaries, but we will work with efforts that help citizens get marijuana arrests expunged from their records. We're doing meaningful work that makes a difference, working with organizations like:

* Counting on Chicago Coalition, ably led by the legendary Donald Dew, President/CEO at Habilitative System, Inc., which was an unrelenting and passionate group of community organizations who moved mountains to make sure every person was counted in the 2020 Census.

* David A. Ansell, MD, MPH, Rush University Medical Center, whom we helped build awareness about the importance for people of color to be involved in COVID vaccine trials.

* Leon Walker, ESQ Managing Partner DL3 Realty, L.P., whose life's passion to develop game-changing properties as a tool to revitalize hard-hit communities by bringing full-service grocery store to a food desert in Englewood.

When you start your own company, you're employed as long as you find the means to sustain yourself. You don't have to take any kind of work. You're in a position to say "no" to work that does not align with your purpose. So instead of being ordinary and saying, "I'll take any work that comes for me," be purpose-driven and intentional. For me, having thirty years of working in diverse communities and working for corporations and brands, starting my own company was step one. But evolving as we approach our ten-year anniversary to only doing work for good means we are serving a cause.

Lessons that Stand Me in Good Stead

It can be scary for a new entrepreneur focused on cash flow to say no to business. The first lesson I learned is to not be afraid, but to be faithful. If you step out on faith, God will meet you where you are. Stay prayerful, and any fear you may have started with becomes the courage of your conviction. Having patience and belief is essential, but underpinning it all is acknowledging and accepting the truth that God is your source. Being prayerful opens the right doors.

The second lesson this journey has taught me is the importance of having a screening process. You must have a compass.

You have to know your core values. That, and a clearly defined mission statement, are the tools I use to make sure the work we select lines up with our core values. To have a purpose-driven life and business, you must have standards and criteria against which prospective clients are evaluated.

Screening the work that you accept can keep you from working for someone you ultimately will end up not respecting, doesn't respect you, or whose actions do not benefit the community. It is also important that your screening process include an out clause. You always want to leave yourself the ability to immediately extricate your business from a situation that could compromise your brand. The worst place you want to be is working for someone whom in the end you won't respect or that you don't think is credible. You never want to compromise your brand.

Learning how to stop doing free work by knowing my worth was huge. I had to learn to be mindful that I was in business and not a corporate ambassador giving people free time and counsel. Knowing my value and my worth and demanding it (because every laborer is worthy of h[er] pay) helps me strike a better balance between how much free versus paid work I do.

It would be misleading to suggest that this evolution has been without its challenges. Cash flow is the scariest part of any new business. Getting steady revenue to cover expenses enough so that I didn't have to go back to work for someone else was the singularly toughest challenge I faced. But I wasn't facing it alone: I stand in the power of faith and prayer.

If I had it to do over again, I would have been more intentional and selective early on. I'd have taken the time to write the vision, establish the criteria for accepting work, and make it real plain. Then I could focus on cultivating bigger, more sustainable business relationships. The more you crystallize what your ideal work looks like, the easier it is to make right decisions on good places to use your talents so that you can be fruitful and multiply.

Parting Tips

Crushing mediocrity is a marathon, not a sprint. Failure is a part of the process. You will make mistakes. Sometimes you win; sometimes you learn. All money isn't good money. But good works lead to good work.

Self-examination is transformational. Do the work. My transformation was spiritual. Seeing life and death, losing my twin and other loved ones showed me that we are not here for a dress rehearsal. Knowing what my talents were and how to properly use my gifts led to clarity of purpose and an understanding of my calling. I am who I am by the grace of God. I'm wired a certain way. And I'm making sure that the folks who work with me have the right spirit as well. Our clients like working with us because we are not transactional people; we can be trusted. Clients call me the Queen of Hearts because they know that I really care. Among my most treasured accolades is a simple sentiment expressed by a hero and mentor of mine, the Rev. Jesse Jackson: "Wynona can be trusted by the community not to bring companies that want to exploit them."

WYNONA REDMOND

Wynona is president of Wyn-Win Communications, Inc., a full-service public relations agency. Her 25-plus years of expertise helping organizations effectively engage their communities, employees and other stakeholders has won Wyn-Win an expanding roster of private and public sector clients.

Wynona crushes mediocrity by choosing assignments that have a clear community benefit: "All money isn't good money" is her mantra. Prior to founding Wyn-Win, she led public affairs and community engagement efforts in both the public and private sector, including Northstar Lottery Group, Dominick's Finer Foods/Safeway, Illinois Department of Children & Family Services, the Chicago Housing Authority and Cook County Hospital.

As president emeritus of the National Black Public Relations Society, Redmond also served as senior advisor on the Public Relations Society of America's board. Additional board service includes the NBC Chicago Community Action Board, the iHeart Media Local Advisory Board, YWCA of Greater Chicago and Greater Chicago Food Depository. Awards and recognitions include the Cook County Juneteenth Committee, National Association of Black Journalists, Matthew House, West Side NAACP, Target Market News, Who's Who In Black Chicago, Chicago Defender Women of Excellence, Top Ladies of Distinction, Today's Black Woman Expo, Rainbow Push Community Award, the YWCA of Metropolitan Chicago and Heroes in the Hood.

She graduated from Loyola University of Chicago with a B.A. in Communications.

Reach her at wynona@wyn-win.com; http://wyn-win.com, FACEBOOK & INSTAGRAM: @wynwincomm.

CHAPTER 8

THE POWER OF SILENCE

BY SHERRY CAPET

"There's something special about a woman who dominates in a man's world. It takes a certain grace, strength, intelligence, fearlessness, and the nerve to never take no for an answer."
~ Rihanna

In the late 1800s, a man by the name of Snowflake Bentley defied everyone in his community by straying from the path he was supposed to take – like being a simple farmer, and instead, he followed his passion. He was the first person to take a photo of a snowflake and preserve the intricate and beautiful design that lasted only moments before disappearing forever.

An innovator of snowflake photography, he advanced the study of meteorology. That one photo was just the first of more than 5,000 he would take in his lifetime. How do I know this story? That man was my great-great-great uncle.

Let's back up, though... who am I?

I am Sherry Capet, executive business and performance coach with more than twenty years of experience providing companies with successful solutions, helping them stay more strategic and focused to more quickly achieve their key performance indicators and manage self-care while building organizational success.

Growing up, I was independent, didn't conform, didn't do what was expected of me, and blazed my own path. In doing this, I was told I was worthless, that no one wanted to listen to me, and if anyone did like me, it was only for how I looked. You can imagine how those words can affect someone, especially a young person. When we are young, we are trying to navigate through the world, figure out who we are, where and if we fit. If we don't, then why and where do we go?

I started working when I was in elementary school. I ran a simple paper route, but it started me on my path. I was very tenacious, disciplined, and curious and wanted to make my own choices, live my own life, and experience every opportunity. I wanted people to realize how smart I was and what I was capable of. What I also learned is that people don't like it when you are smart, especially a woman in the presence of a man. I was told to dumb myself down and at times to even go to the back of the line or the room so that the men could be taken care of first.

When I was in college, I went to school full time and worked full time. I decided to apply at ESPN. I found out the name of the director of an entry-level position and sent him my resume almost every day. I did this until I received a phone call, and I remember the voice on the other end saying, "Who are you and how did you get my name?"

I said, "My name is Sherry, and I am going to work for you." After that very brief conversation, I continued to send my resume, and eventually, I received a call asking me to come in for an interview. I went for the interview, and it went great. At the end I was told thanks but that I wouldn't be hired. I asked why. They said, "You're in college full time; it would be too much for you to work here full time as well." I looked the interviewer right in the eyes and said, "I appreciate that, but I will see you soon." They said I seemed confident for someone who was just told they weren't going to get the job. I was sure they would hire me, and six months later, that's exactly what happened. I received a call offering me the job, and I took it.

Once I arrived, I remember being told, "Welcome to a man's world. I hope you can handle it." At the time, I didn't know what that meant. I was new; this was my first corporate job. I had little to no experience, and I wasn't afraid to say yes to the opportunity. I also didn't know I was about to blaze another path, being a woman in a "man's world." I learned quickly and loved what I did. I went to school full time during the day and worked second (sometimes third) shift at night, doing my homework on break, during quiet times and around my work schedule. My life consisted of school, homework, making great friends, learning a lot about what I wanted in life and being curious about what was yet to come.

I've traveled and learned from amazing executives, both women and men. I remember one of the men saying they would rather have women be in the lead, management, and executive positions. They said women weren't treated fairly and to stand up for what I believed. They said that women were brilliant and better business leaders than most men. I was learning what this meant, and it made me more curious.

I took my first management position managing a staff of men, one of whom made it known he didn't like working for a woman, and he refused to do so. I had firsts in many areas of business and pioneering new ideas that many thought were impossible. Being told my ideas and thoughts would never happen, that the world was going to stay as it was and that I should give up made me want it more, and I didn't take "no" for an answer.

As I continued through my corporate adventure, I looked for ways to make a difference. I started working virtually in 2004, and I was heavily criticized. I was laughed at, told this would never happen and I would never succeed. What was I thinking? Yet, here we are in 2021 working virtually! It has become the new normal, and businesses realize that virtual and hybrid work options create better lives for employees.

I removed negativity and surrounded myself with people who are positive, challenging, and uplifting. When I encounter negativity, I consider the lesson I can take from it. Is there an opportunity? To grow? To learn? To succeed and help others succeed at living their dreams?

Looking back and thinking about all I did to overcome, I realize just how hard it was. While people were conforming, I was alone. I was refusing to be a follower and wanted to be a leader. I was standing up for what I believed, and I wasn't letting anyone stop me. It was very lonely, and I would find myself crying, not understanding why but knowing it was right and that I would do great things. I didn't have support; I had people saying they were intimidated; they didn't know how to talk to me, and they wanted a "yes" person. Well, that wasn't me, and I wasn't going to change to make someone feel better.

Every time I was kicked down, I got back up. Every time I was told "You can't do that," I said, "Watch me." When people who were supposed to be my friends told me that I was worthless and that no one wanted what I had to offer, that I would never amount to anything, that I wasn't even worthy of their friendship and that I needed to stay at the level I was at and do what they were doing because that was right, I told them goodbye. As hard as that was, as lonely as it was and as scary as it was, I wasn't letting fear stop me. I was letting it motivate me. I started reading more, undertaking more personal development, learning from executives and leaders. I didn't want to be the smartest person in the room, and I never wanted to stop learning. Don't be silenced; stand up for what you know and what is right.

Stay strong; don't let other people kick you down. Don't let other people tell you that you will never achieve your dreams. Don't let that negative mindset take over. Be the leader, the trailblazer for others who are looking to break those barriers. If you don't have an answer, find it. If you want to do something, do it. If you want to learn something, learn it. No one is stopping you, but you. You *always* have a choice in life.

As I reflect on the stories I heard as a child, things my grandfather had shown me that my uncle had created, and I acknowledge his traits and accomplishments, I see a lot of that within me and know he is one of the many influences I had in my life. I have that same spirit to blaze my own path, to refuse to conform, to think ahead of my time, challenge the status quo, and follow my curiosity and passion.

When they say no, I say why not?

When they say it can't be done, I say let's do it.

If a man could in 1865 take a photograph of snowflakes and blaze a path in meteorology and photography during a time when this wasn't supposed to be possible, what is stopping you from blazing your own path?

48

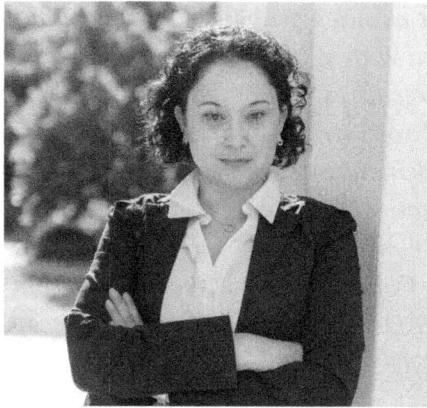

SHERRY CAPET

Sherry Capet is a business development professional with more than seventeen years of experience providing companies with successful solutions, helping them stay more strategic and focused to achieve their key performance indicators more quickly and manage self-care while building organizational success. She has a solid understanding of project management and operations and is a skilled communicator and innovative thinker who identifies more efficient ways of growing company assets by recommending new processes and procedures to maximize efficiency and increase productivity. She has worked with some of the most significant corporate executives including leaders of thirteen of the Fortune 100 and nine of the Fortune 500 companies.

As a young single mother, she was homeless. She overcame cancer and lost her fiancé to suicide. She knows things happen for us, not to us, and everything that happened has made her stronger. Sherry knows the value of time and how sacred the small moments are. When she decided to work virtually in 2004, she was laughed at but persevered. Immersing herself in the global opportunities that were being presented allowed her to become a success both personally and professionally while never missing a moment of her son's life, making irreplaceable memories, expanding her knowledge, continuing her education, and building her experience.

Sherry has vast knowledge about a variety of industries and has consulted with White House officials, film and music entertainment executives, major league athletes, medical professionals, IT executives, and media and entertainment litigators on implementing strategies and techniques while building solid, motivational teams that think outside the box.

Connect at www.sherrycapet.com
FACEBOOK: @sherryangeliquecapet
INSTAGRAM: @sherry_angelique_capet

CHAPTER 9

I WAS MADE FOR THIS

BY SUZAN BROWN

My name is Suzan Brown, I was born in Chicago Illinois, but raised in Grand Rapids Michigan. I am an entrepreneurial woman, and this is how I crushed mediocrity and disrupted the status quo.

The year was 2005. One night I got a call from my oldest daughter. She was crying hysterically, telling me to come get her kids because she felt like she was having a nervous breakdown. I tried talking to her to calm her down so that I could hear what she was saying. We were in a different city, so I tried to reassure her that I would be there, for her to just hold on. Before I could get to her, she had already called Child Protective Services to come and pick up her kids. My daughter was going through a rough time, and I knew that. I really wanted her to live where her father and I were, but unfortunately, she made other plans. She had been diagnosed with debilitating diseases: lupus and myasthenia gravis. Her symptoms continued to get worse. When her doctor gave her the final diagnosis of myasthenia gravis, surgery was her next battle. She was suffering, and there was nothing I could do about it.

When I got to her, things were already out of my hands. CPS had given my grandchildren to a close relative. When I asked about getting custody of them, I found out that my name had been placed on a central registry   because of my addiction to crack cocaine in 1984. In all those years, I never knew that I had been placed on a central registry for neglect. Also, I could not get my grandchildren because my relatives were fighting to keep them, and the children were already temporary wards of the courts. My daughter and I found ourselves fighting against

51

those we thought loved us. My daughter only wanted someone to help her, not to take her children away from her.

Eventually, the courts awarded my grandchildren to an immediate family member. I have seven brothers and three sisters, and I promise you, the bond was unbreakable, or so I thought.

My relatives' hatred for me took a toll on the entire family. It took a toll on my daughter's health as well. My daughter could not see her children or visit them. My daughter's heart was broken, but she continued to fight for her children.

The same month that her appeal was granted, she passed away from her infirmities. I tried to continue where she left off. I was told that her rights died with her, and as a grandparent I had no rights. So here I was faced with the thing I feared the most. Just imagine losing your first born and not being able to see the children she gave birth to. Imagine one of your siblings raising your grandchildren as their own. It is the worst kind of pain imaginable.

My first encounter with CPS began in 1984 when my children became temporary wards of the court. In 1983 my fiancé – now husband -- was sent to prison for 14.5 years for a crime he committed. I was left alone to raise five children on my own. Within a year my life spiraled out of control. Depression set in, and I turned to drugs to ease the pain. Leaving my children with family became easy.

Eventually, my family called CPS and that's when reality began to set in. My life became a nightmare. I went all in with drugs and prostitution. Leaving my children with family was no longer a choice. I sold everything I had to get the drugs I thought I needed.

I got tired of being sick and tired and being labeled a crackhead. There I was again, alone in my own home, but this time I was ready to make a sound decision to fight for my children. The courts said that for me to gain custody of my children, I had to complete all their requirements. I was sent to a women's rehab center in Detroit, Michigan, for eleven months. It was there that I learned how to live a clean and sober life. It was there that I defeated and crushed the status quo that says, "Once a drug addict, always a drug addict." It took eleven months for me to do it, but I did it, and sure enough, I was awarded all five of my children. Doing just enough to get by or just enough to take care of my children had to end. I received counseling for my depression. I removed all the toxic so-called friends in my life. To live a life worthy of becoming all that God made me to be, I had to completely change my outlook. Just because I felt alone did not mean that I was alone. It took years for me to face Suzan and her insecurities. Drugs were not my problem; I was my problem. Drugs were only the Band-Aid I used to hide my true self.

The programs the courts required me to complete set me on a course that would change my life forever. The parenting classes taught me how to be a better mother to my children. The NA and AA meetings supplied me with the tools needed to live a sober life after I left the treatment facility. I remember during an NA meeting someone in the group suggested that I get a higher power to help sustain me in my walk of sobriety. I chose Jesus Christ to be that higher power. I began to attend church with some of the women who were residents. My whole outlook on life had changed during the time I spent at the women's facility.

Back to the future, in 2006 my daughter passed away from her infirmities. I felt so defeated after my daughter died. I truly forgot about the fighter within me. I gave up, and this vicious cycle continued.

In 2011 I was faced with the same dilemma I thought I had crushed with my children. I had won the battle for custody of my children, but the war was still on. My son's children became temporary wards of the courts because of the lifestyle he and his wife chose to live. Listen, just because you defeated mediocrity once does not mean you won't have other battles to contend with. This time my husband and I were ready and well able to intervene.

God allowed my name to be expunged from the central

registry. Amen. The courts terminated my son's and his estranged wife's rights. We fought for our grandsons, and it was a battle. I remembered how I crushed the lies I was told years ago. There is a saying I started repeating to myself once I became clean and sober: "I was made for this." I've always disrupted the status quo. I was often told that I needed a psychiatrist or that I cry too much, which might have been true. But I did not allow that to stop me from what I knew I needed to do. Once I realized I'd been defeating the status quo all my life, the fight was on.

So, I was ready to crush the CPS system. For three generations CPS had been tormenting my life. Not anymore. This system has some awesome qualities, but it also has a lot of flaws. I was determined to make a difference in the lives of my grandchildren by any means necessary. I would not allow CPS to dictate the future of my grandchildren. My husband and I were successful in getting custody of my grandsons.

Today we, and not CPS, are raising our grandchildren. It's been almost eight years, and they are doing really well. We're also senior pastors of the New Breed Church in Grand Rapids, Michigan.

I have a women's ministry entitled Sisters Celebrating Sisters/ The Deborah Company. I just launched a class called Basic Training For Prophets, and I am pursuing one of my passions, Esther's Home of Transformation for Single Women & Children. This year I will complete my doctoral degree in theology. I have no time for mediocrity, and I'm definitely disrupting the status quo on all levels. Just remember: you were made for this. Whatever your struggle is, you were created with the storm in mind. The God I serve has given me everything I need to be successful in life. I know if I can do it, I promise, you can too.

MAKE THIS YOUR DAILY DECLARATION:

Clearly, I am an entrepreneurial woman disrupting the status quo and crushing mediocrity.

PROPHETESS SUZAN BROWN

Prophetess Suzan Brown is and end-time prophet whom God has raised up to speak a word of life and liberation to His ecclesia (Church), especially women.

After Prophetess Suzan was set free from a lifestyle of crack cocaine and prostitution, God commissioned her to speak into the lives of all those who are bound by the enemy's devices. Prophetess Suzan is heavily involved in prophetic service, prophetic intercession, healing, and deliverance. She ministers in homeless shelters, rehab facilities, tent crusades, seminars, and workshops, and serves as a keynote speaker at numerous conferences. Prophetess Suzan is one of the collaborative authors of "Hidden Impact, Unveiled For Kingdom Purpose" and has authored her first book, "My Testimony: The Day The Deliverer Showed Up." In 2005, the late Apostle William T. Nichols and Apostle Veter Nichols Shaw ordained Suzan Brown and placed her in the office of prophetess.

Prophetess Suzan is the CEO and founder of Sisters Celebrating Sisters, Sistertalk Broadcast & Basic Training For Prophets.

In May 2016 Suzan Brown and her husband, Perfecto, were ordained and installed in the office of pastors. Together they now pastor the New Breed Church in Grand Rapids, Michigan. Prophetess Suzan is pursuing her passion to open Esther's Home of Transformation for Single Women & Children.

Pastors Suzan and Perfecto Brown are the proud parents of five beautiful children. Together they have twenty-one precious grandchildren and two beautiful great-grandchildren. She gives God all the glory, honor, and praise.

EMAIL: sisterscelebratingsisters@gmail.com
WEBSITE: suzanbrownministries.com
FACEBOOK: @prophetess.suzan
INSTAGRAM: @prophetesssuzan

CHAPTER 10

DIVINE STRATEGY
IT'S EXACTLY THE WAY IT'S SUPPOSED TO BE.

BY SHERRI ALLEN-REEVES

It was the morning of December 31, 2015, New Year's Eve; I was home on medical leave recuperating from surgery. I received a phone call from my colleague and office mate, who said, "I just got fired today, and you would have to if you had come to work." My work had always centered on helping people be of service to others. This job was no different; I was helping single men and women who were transitioning from being homeless to being housed.

At that moment, several questions came to mind: is this true? Did I get fired from the job that I poured my heart into and for which I often sacrificed my health and family? And, why would this person (and not my boss) call me?

I was overwhelmed with emotions, and my heart was pounding. It was as if I could feel my blood rushing through my veins. I kept looking at the phone, thinking this couldn't be true. I was alternately angry, confused, and worried. My employer wouldn't fire me on New Year's Eve, especially while I was on medical leave. They like me; I have always been that committed employee. With courage and anxiety, I picked up the phone and began dialing the number to my workplace. I had to hear this for myself, directly from my boss. With every ring of the phone, I became more anxious, and it felt like my stomach had hit the floor and was doing flips. Finally, my boss answered the phone, and in her usual monotone voice, she announced herself. I responded with a fake cheery-sounding hello. I explained that I was calling because I had heard that I had been fired. Her response, which appeared to lack remorse, care, or compassion, was, "Yes, as you know, we are having budget issues. As a result, we are restructuring, and I had to let you go. I sent your letter to your email." Which one? My email at work? The one that I don't have remote access to! Who does that? I wasn't angry that I was fired from a job that I had had for ten years, five months, and fifteen days -- a place where I did for others oftentimes more than I did for myself. I encouraged them to go to the doctor, to really take care of their health. I assisted in reunification with their estranged families. I encouraged them to go back to school to obtain both secondary and post-secondary education, and I helped them get their finances on track. I always felt respected and admired by the residents, so it was difficult to understand why I was fired and the way it was done.

When I finally gained my footing, I thought, "Well, this must be exactly how it was supposed to be."

I had wanted to leave that job for years. I often felt unappreciated by leadership, and my being a fierce advocate for the residents often disrupted the status quo.

Also, there were beliefs and adages that I held onto that made it impossible for me to quit. For instance, I thought, "You don't quit a job without having a new one" or "As long as pay doesn't change, you don't either" or the classic one: "You can't quit your good job." Those were tapes that continually played in my head, and I believe they had me stuck.

But God! God did for me what I could not do for myself; He released me and disrupted the status quo. The year 2016 started with my having no job and no plan and no clear ideas about my future. So much self-worth and values were tied to my job, taking care of my family, caring about what others thought about me, and what I had or had not accomplished in life.

I also began the year asking God, "Is it the way it's supposed to be?"

I had to have a major shift in my thinking, and the new year became my time of transformation and gathering of information. I began to focus on my personal growth, seek my purpose, enlarge my territory, expand my worldview, and cultivate new relationships.

I had to change the order of things I valued from a job: family, fitting in, and being accepted. I had rarely put myself first, and when I did, I felt guilty. Now I enjoy implementing personal growth strategies, increasing my self-confidence, embracing spirituality, the joys of happiness, and forgiveness.

As for personal growth, that's where I discovered myself through the power of acknowledgment. For years people would say to me, "Sherry, you are so motivating," or "Sherry, you are beautiful;" "You look wonderful in that dress," and I would just shrug it off because I didn't believe it. I have now learned that the power of acknowledgment is receiving. Amazingly, the power works both ways, because when you accept acknowledgment, you embrace and become the words of the giver, and they get the pleasure of seeing you accept their gift. People can see things you can't or won't see about yourself. So often, we're stuck in the stories of our past, and when people acknowledge us, it's hard to believe. For years I took for granted the power of words and their impact on me. However, I fully understand that words are said, and whoever says them has only the energy or meaning that I allow. I get to choose if they heal or hurt.

My appearance also trapped me as a woman so consumed about how I looked. I mostly saw myself as the stereotypical big, Black, and loud woman. I never saw myself as really beautiful and often sought relationships that validated my opinion of myself.

Today you will tell by my bald head I have embraced my self-esteem and own my beauty and confidence. For years I covered my balding head with H.I.B.: Hair I Bought. Today I love my authentic self; I stand proudly loving myself as bald, Black, and beautiful.

My spirituality has increased. I am clearer today about who I am while continuing to seek a higher level of clarity to walk in my divine purpose. I have always run away from ministry, all the time not realizing I was living it. I fully understand today that I am a servant after God's own heart. With that knowledge, I am happier with my life today, creating my future, living my truth, and discovering my voice.

I continue to work on forgiveness; I am grateful for my boss who fired me, because, without her, this transformation might not have happened. I went from being an unemployed case manager to becoming a non-profit executive. In addition, I serve on several community boards. I advocate for those locally and nationally who have been homeless. I am unapologetic about my opinions until new knowledge is learned and accepted.

I have forgiven those who have harmed me because it no longer serves me to hold on to that harm. But, more importantly, I forgave myself for not believing in myself and not permitting myself to love myself the way I am and the way I am not. I am no longer striving for perfection. I was born perfect, just the way God designed me.

Today, I practice living by five agreements written by Don Miguel Ruiz: I am impeccable with my word; I don't take anything personally; I don't make assumptions; I always do my best, and I am learning to be skeptical, but also to listen. This journey has taught me that every day is an opportunity to learn something different. I am not the same person I was in 2016, nor am I the same person I was yesterday. Every day God grants me new mercies, and the lessons of yesterday, today, and tomorrow are exactly the way they are supposed to be.

I often strived to become this idea of perfection, when in reality, perfect is how I was born. I compared my happiness, my looks, my accomplishments with those of other people, when the truth of the matter is I was measuring myself against someone else's yardstick.

For me, disrupting the status quo and crushing mediocrity means I will no longer make myself small to have others feel big. It means using my voice and my words to make a difference. It means challenging myself daily to learn something different or to meet someone new. It really means I get to say who I am and how I create my life.

I now create my life through my word; I get to say what works or doesn't work for me.

I now walk in my power, because I know my value and worth.

I now know who I am, and I now know I am enough.

It is a divine strategy and exactly the way it's supposed to be.

SHERRI ALLEN-REEVES

Sherri Allen-Reeves is a leading-edge thinker, speaker, and author who, as associate director of Matthew House in Chicago, Illinois, has spent over thirty-five years providing support services to thousands. Matthew House operates as a support service center for the homeless. Sherri has facilitated hundreds of workshops for life skills, vision boards, and public speaking. As the founder of the Renaissance Bronzeville Toastmasters Club, she has participated in several speech competitions and placed in them all. She has provided coaching and mentoring to hundreds, and she wants to utilize the skills as she's gained over thirty-five years to create transformation globally. Sherri has been trained in effective coaching in communication skills, qualifying her to help others transform their lives. Sherri also brings to her work her life experience of being married for thirty-two years, raising three children, and being a grandparent to six grandchildren.

DISRUPTING THE STATUS QUO

EMAIL: Sherrispeaks1@gmail.com
FACEBOOK: Sherri Allen-Reeves
INSTAGRAM: 4realsherri

CHAPTER 11

DISRUPTIVE OR DETERMINED?

BY CHERYL THIBAULT

"I learned that courage was not the absence of fear, but the triumph over it. The brave man is not he who does not feel afraid, but he who conquers that fear." – Nelson Mandela

I am Cheryl Thibault. I was born in Regina, Saskatchewan, a city in the middle of Canada. I now reside on beautiful Vancouver Island, British Columbia, Canada. I am an entrepreneurial multi-business owner, educator, podcast host, author, and game changer in the beauty Industry. I have crushed mediocrity more than once and would like to invite you to enjoy the inspiring story of my traumatic yet remarkable life journey. Discover what it took for me to independently go from a beaten-down, divorced, broke single mom to owning a global business that helps people all over the world fulfill their dreams.

I was the middle child with an older and a younger brother. My parents were not affectionate and rarely said, "I Love you," so I guess you could say I craved attention, and the rebellious side of me started at a very young age. I would take my infant brother out of his crib and hide him under the bed, then jump into the crib and call for my mom to come find me. I was three years old.

I left home at thirteen to make my own way in life. I quickly found out that it wasn't as much fun or as easy as I thought. I always was a bit of an instigator, trying so hard to fit in and be cool. I was arrested at fourteen years old for selling drugs in a bar. The police took me home to my parents because I was too young to go to jail.

I was a high school dropout, pregnant at sixteen, married at seventeen, pregnant at eighteen, and I divorced my alcoholic husband when I was nineteen. These life events gave me the determination to succeed.

We were fortunate to purchase our first home when I was seventeen. But my husband's drinking took priority and escalated into violence. The mortgage never got paid, and we ended up losing the home and moving into low-income housing. I could not raise my children under these conditions. I was forced to consider my options.

My childhood dream was to be in the beauty industry, so I began researching how I could make this dream a reality. The closest school I found was 400 miles away, and I knew the only way forward for us was for me to leave my children with my parents and go away to school.

I saved enough money selling stitchery at night through a home party plan to pay for my course, and off I went. Leaving my children behind was the hardest thing I had to do. I saw the big picture, and I focused on the outcome. With my goal in mind, I went to school both day and night and completed in half the time, with honors.

I came home and was so excited to be reunited with my family, only to find myself that same afternoon moving into a transition house for abused families. My children and I lived there until I had earned enough money to rent a new home.

While working in a salon, I soon saw that I was not the only one who dreamed of a career in this industry. Did everyone have to leave their families and go away to school? What if there were a local school? I saw the need and got busy putting all the pieces in place to make this happen. Within two years of graduating, I had opened the first school of its kind in my province. I was twenty-two years old and determined to make a difference.

Life was busy as a single mom, but I had to keep my priorities in sight and work toward my goals. Was I tired? Absolutely. Was I broke? Yes. Was I determined? You better believe I was. Was I motivated? I had two kids to feed -- what choice did I have?

My school became very successful. I had a three-year wait list. I hired an office administrator and later learned she had been secretly photocopying all my student and client files. She was set to open a school of her own with the intent to bankrupt me. She did partially succeed; she did open a competitive school. I owe my continued success to my loyal students and clients for believing in me. My parents taught me to treat others with honesty and integrity, and you will always win.

During this same time frame, I was working very long hours when I got a call from the hospital. This was the call a mother never wants to hear: "Your daughter has been hit by a truck and is in emergency; come immediately."

I distinctly recall walking into the emergency room to see my beautiful six-year-old lying on a pillow with her pretty face covered in blood. While a nurse was suctioning blood out of her mouth, I could hear her teeth going down the hose.

She looked up at me with her beautiful blue eyes and said, "It could have been worse; it could have been a bus!" What a positive attitude this little girl had. She was blessed with a miracle and came out of the hospital that same week. Her older brother expressed his happiness by popping wheelies with her in the wheelchair down the hallway. I always say you don't meet my son; you experience him. He is quite a character.

Throughout this tumultuous ordeal, I was involved with another man. He was not a drinker, but I faced a worse nightmare. He was extremely abusive. I went to see a social worker for help and guidance to remove my children from that situation, only to be told "now that we know what is going on in your home, we must remove the children. If they go back to that home, as of 5:00 today, they will be placed in foster care."

What did I just hear? My kids, taken away from me? Never. I picked up the kids from school and moved back to my parents' home, where I stayed for months. When I did move into our next home, I had to have 24/7 police protection for both me and my kids. I was "strongly encouraged" to leave town, so I was forced to close my very successful business to protect my family.

The kids and I packed my small car and moved over 1,000 miles away to start a new life again.

I had no job and very little money, so we lived in a tent in a campground for months until I found a house to rent. I worked three jobs and was absolutely exhausted. I remember the night I just could not go on. I remembered the book One Day At A Time, which I read when healing from the alcoholic first marriage, but that was not enough. I could not make it through the day. I wrote one minute at a time, and finally I knew if I could get through one second at a time, this too would pass.

Two years later, the kids and I moved to this beautiful Island where we all live today. As I write this, my son is forty-three and married to a beautiful woman. My daughter is forty-one, the wife of an amazing man and the mother of three fabulous children.

In 2006 I was in a tragic motorcycle accident and spent almost a year in a wheelchair and several years in therapy. There were many very dark days for me, and at one time I wrote a goodbye letter to my kids. As I was completing this letter, I remembered other times when I felt I could not go on, *but I did anyway*!

I was forced to be creative, and I developed a new way to educate my students. I began using videos. I started to educate through the use of DVDs and then took the classes completely online. Becoming the first person in North America (possibly the world) to offer online classes for esthetics and nail technology was a most outstanding achievement. My company is now helping students all over the world fulfill their dreams. I have since founded other schools, several spas, and warehouses. I have trademarked and branded my own line of nail, skin, body, and makeup products called Spa One.

My personal mission is to heal; inspire; and serve, using my life, energy, love, and intuition to create change. My life has become one of caring for others.

"People will forget what you said; people will forget what you did, but people will never forget how you made them feel."
-Maya Angelou.

The importance of what is of true value does not hold a price tag.
Strive for your dreams; they're never too small or too big.
Follow your heart; listen to that tender voice inside and do what
you believe is right. Never give up – even if it means making a
sideways or a backward move; you will always go forward again.

Live your life with purpose and passion; follow your heart –
Keep Creating

My vision is to create a heart-led world where people come
together with love, understanding, compassion, and kindness
for the good of everyone.

CHERYL THIBAULT

*Cheryl Thibault is a visionary, entrepreneur, multi-business
owner, educator, influencer, and game changer in the beauty
industry. Cheryl is a student of life who will never stop growing
and learning. She is assertive and an uncompromising beauty
professional and has been for over 40 years. As founder/owner
of beauty spas and education centers throughout Canada since
1981, Cheryl produced one of her greatest achievements, her
creation, Mirage Spa Education Inc., which is a global beauty
school that teaches nail technology, esthetics, spa therapy, and
other related topics. The creation was a hidden gem, with its
100% online platform unknown to the industry at the time. Self-*

described as a single mom "who did" (overcoming incredible life challenges thrown her way) and a bad-ass mom "who still does" (not letting anything stand in the way of her dreams), Cheryl continues her mission to provide opportunities and empower others to change their lives in a positive way. She has been invited to judge several prestigious nail competitions throughout North America and is an author and co-author. She is penning a series of books dedicated to telling her life story, overcoming struggles, and gaining life and career success. Cheryl is hosting a podcast, The Walk of Life, which will cover many other amazing people on their walks of life. She is a true trailblazer who has been creating businesses and educating for over 40 years. She actively integrates love, understanding, and compassion into all areas of her life as she influences thousands around the world to carry that forward.

WEBSITE: misscheryl.com
FACEBOOK: @cheryltbo
INSTAGRAM: CherylThibault1

misscheryl.com
misscheryl.com

CHAPTER 12

SCREENSHOT TO SUCCESS

BY GINA LAMAR

This chapter is dedicated to my sisters, Terri and Cathy.

My name is Gina Lamar, but my birth certificate says Baby Girl Burke. According to my middle sister, they found me in the garbage can. She just hasn't gotten over my being born; it's been fifty-five years. Our biological father died one week after my second birthday. My mother would be widowed for almost ten years until Sid Lee walked in and changed our lives forever… we'll just color him father.

After 1978, my life was grounded in love and stability, not that there wasn't plenty of love before then, but this was a different kind of love, one that every person should experience at least once in life. My parents worked very hard to provide for us. My dad always taught me to do what I must so that later I could do what I want. It was confusing at first, but the more I did chores without being told, and the more I excelled in school, the more I understood it. Though that acceleration was long and slow, it took me eleven years to complete undergrad and get a bachelor's degree. Don't ask why it took so long; just know that I finished.

I started graduate school in fall of 1999 working on a Master of Public Health degree. I remember stopping by my parents' house and sharing my two A's with them, and my dad said, "Look, Mary, she gets an A the first time when she's paying for the classes." The following month, in January 2000, I would bury my parents in a double-casket funeral.

If anyone remembers Y2K, we all heard the world was ending at the stroke of midnight. But I was convinced the world was ending when my mother died suddenly of heart failure on January 10, and my father was put into hospice and died six days later, January 16, from cancer. We waited until the following Saturday, January 22, to hold mass and bury them side by side.

I was broken, devastated, hopeless, and scared as hell. Clearly, someone had gotten the dates mixed up, and Y2K was happening right there in real time because my world had just ended. God took my mother and my father.

I went back to work within days of my parents' funeral, trying to get my life back to some normalcy, just calmly waiting on Y2K to take us all away to wherever it had taken my parents.

I am a case manager for people living with HIV. I was in the middle of working with a 19-year-old Black female who was on her second child and did not understand why she had to come to our clinic for this pregnancy. As I explained why she was referred to me, she broke down sobbing, and I broke down with her. I was sent home and made to take leave to truly grieve my major loss. To this day I will stand by the fact that this 19-year-old's new reality was why I broke down and not because of my personal pain.

Months later I received a call from my professor. I remember squawking at the very thought of his calling me about some damn class I had not finished. He calmly extended his condolences once again and then firmly stated that he was looking for my registration for the fall of 2000. I rolled my neck and my eyes as I screamed, "Don't you know I lost my mother and my father?"

He said "Yes, the very parents who died thinking you were pursuing a master's degree. Please register as soon as possible." My parents were now my angels working in my favor. It feels as though my life took off. I was dating again; my career took off; my sisters and I were bonded now more than ever before. But all the while I was dying slowly inside from the pain of missing my first and truest cheerleaders. My parents died with me in their hearts, hopes, wills, wonders, pockets, and credit report. I would spend the next twenty years deep in an addiction that I could never truly admit: I was addicted to gambling. I always justified my nonsense with the fact that I had no children, no mortgage, and no car note. I was lying to myself.

My career took me all over the world of HIV, from testing, to teaching, to managing, to finally owning NEFUSE Case Management & Training Services. In June 2020, I left my "good county job" and opened the doors to my very own case management and training agency where I could serve my community my way. I could meet my people in any place on any level and truly connect with them and refer them to trusted Black providers. I didn't step out on faith. I *jumped* off the cliff and into the arms of faith-filled women who broke my fall at every turn -- paying bills, covering tabs, never allowing me to feel less than while I had no money.

"To know me is to love me or not... I don't think anyone really hates me... at least, I don't think so."

I'm an energy person. If your energy is all off, then I'm going to keep it moving... the hell away from you. I'm always smiling and upbeat. It's how I fight my depression. Oh, yeah, I get really depressed, like hospitalization depressed. Fall is my favorite season, but those blinds have to stay open to combat those demons.

Disrupting the status quo is not only a hard task, it's also a hard concept. Humans tend to love negative energy. When you enter a room smiling and say hello, you might get a few hellos back, but if you enter a room cussin' and fussin', 88% of that room will get on board, even if it's just to complain about the way you entered the room. (By the way, I totally made that statistic up.)

They don't even realize that they, too, have just jumped on the negative bandwagon and are headed down the highway of complacency, mediocrity, low morale, and good ol' status quo. I would like for this chapter to be the one to remind you of just how easy it is to become the status quo and how much easier it is to disrupt it.

We can indeed change that narrative. If we could take just nine minutes per day to love on ourselves through kindness, patience, and grace, it would absolutely change the outcome of our day, and over time, the outcome of our lives.

Take nine minutes of your day, and in those minutes create a space that is clean, orderly, and quiet. Even if you live with others in a small space, start in the bathroom, but remember to clean it, clear the clutter, and tune out the others. This might require either getting up earlier or staying up later, but I promise you, it will be worth it. You are creating a pattern of habits that build into a routine that transforms into a lifestyle and becomes your way of life.

Here are a few steps:
1. Write out the life you truly want... whether it's having the job of your dreams or being married to a billionaire
2. Decide how you'll get that life... hard work, investments, inheritance, open a business
3. Begin... just start working toward your goal
4. Write your daily tasks... my alarm reads "rise-pray-slay"
5. Down to the basics... literally jot down tasks: pray, make the bed, drink water, bathroom, stretch, or simply sit still for nine minutes and clear your mind.
6. Read your schedule for the day... schedule *everything*
7. Plan your meals and your outfits
8. List your tasks and include pushing the limit, a kind gesture, smiling, and cleaning your phone case
9. No sleep until your list is complete, including your next day's list

I am the queen of procrastination; I must change that mindset. I opened my agency, then Aunt Corona (Covid-19) showed up, making the arrival of Aunt Flo (a menstrual cycle) a party in comparison.

I almost backed out, but then I began seeing the very health inequities I was fighting against manifest all around me. Opening a Black woman-owned agency became a *must* instead of a plus.

This has been a very trying year, but if it was going to be, it was up to me. My sisters and my sister circles have carried me far and shown me just how supportive women can be when you allow yourself to accept help.

I took those very nine steps and made them my creed in order to remain self-employed and truly help my community. I am willing to drive old cars and not have cable so that I can lower the number of Black women infected/impacted by HIV, disrupting those statistics.

GINA LAMAR

Gina Lamar is a public health expert and HIV training specialist. She is owner of Monday Night Mingle and NEFUSE Case Management and Training Services.

Gina appears quarterly in various media, discussing statistics for HIV and sexually transmitted diseases. She has been featured in Crain's Chicago Business.

Her program, The Mingling Minute, airs every Monday at 9:30 a.m. and features an expert who answers questions about healthy relations and sexually transmitted diseases

Gina moderates candid community conversations every first Tuesday, facilitating dialogue on Black health and highlighting inequities and disparities.

Every third Monday, Gina appears on the Xavia Fox Morning Show, where she says she does "a little Monday morning quarterbacking about barebacking."

www.ginalamar.com
EMAIL: gina@MondayNightMingle.com
INSTAGRAM: @MondayNightMingle
FACEBOOK: gina.lamar.3

CHAPTER 13

MEDIOCRITY, A THIEF OF ENTREPRENEURSHIP

BY TOYA L. GARNER

My name is Toya Garner, and I'm from a suburban town not too far from Chicago, Illinois. I am an entrepreneurial woman who has crushed mediocrity, and I want to share with you my story about how I recognized that mediocrity is a thief of entrepreneurship.

In 1999, I opened my first business, a bath and body store. I'd always wanted to make women look and feel good about themselves, so I thought this was the perfect way to do so. I was excited and so hopeful about making my mark and changing women's lives with my products. I got my business license, secured a business loan, leased a storefront on a high-traffic street, ordered my inventory and store fixtures, and hired a contractor to do my store's build out.

Everything was looking up until it all fell. The loan amount wasn't nearly enough money to open a retail store. I had just enough money to cover my rent, build-out costs/labor, inventory, and absolutely no money left over for marketing. My inventory was held up for two months due to a severe blizzard on the east coast. The first contractor I hired took my money, never started working, and bailed out. Then to add insult to injury, I had the nerve to try to open my store in the month of December. I thought that I could capitalize on the holiday shoppers, but I missed the entire season. By the way, the inventory finally arrived in February. Go figure!

I was devastated and humiliated. I left a good-paying job with the offer of a promotion to chase a dream that had me sitting day after day in my store with not one customer entering through the door. Well, why would they? I had little to nothing to sell. My shelves looked worse than Old Mother Hubbard's cupboards. I felt like a complete loser. This was an all-time low. It was time to move out of the storefront and, thank God, the owners didn't hold me to the lease since I'd fixed up the place so nicely. It was in move-in ready condition, and I believe the realtor felt sorry for me. Either way, she got paid. I gave away all my shelving, point-of-sale system, and remaining inventory and then filed for bankruptcy.

I vowed to never start another business. I did not want to go through this experience again. Who wants to look and feel like a failure? Not me! I was taking the safe route from now on, and if that meant living a life of mediocrity, then so be it. Even though I gave up and felt like mediocrity was safe, God had a different plan. He never gave up on me, and even my husband tried to encourage me to start again. I wasn't trying to hear either of them. I no longer wanted to be identified as an entrepreneur. I was comfortable working on the job, coming home, and taking care of my family. Well, at least I thought I was comfortable. My purpose and destiny to be an entrepreneur was calling me. They would always find a way to rise up and push me to do something that challenged my mindset, fears, and limitations.

Mediocrity is defined as the quality or state of being mediocre, ordinary, so-so. It's a comfortable place. No pressure, no stress, no drive or push to be better or greater. It can be a struggle to keep your entrepreneurial spirit alive and thriving when you have been hit with devastating circumstances and situations that knock you down. But as the saying goes, when you get knocked down seven times, get up eight, and that's what I did. I had to realize that mediocrity was not my destiny and purpose. I knew that God wanted me to be an entrepreneur as well as a prophet. I had to make up my mind that I was going to defeat mediocrity and redirect my focus to the passion, purpose, and destiny for my life in ministry and as an entrepreneur.

About two years after my business failed, my husband and I stepped out in faith and started our ministry. The Lord began to put me in situations where the anointing and skills He gave me as an entrepreneur began to take center stage. I would try to hide it, and no matter how I tried to stay in a place of mediocrity concerning business, I would find myself involved with projects that pushed me to operate as an entrepreneur. I have always had a heart to serve and wanted to please God with my life, so to help my friends and family for free with their business ventures and projects was not a problem. But there came a time when God would impress upon me to start a business. The answer was always, "No, God. I am not doing that again." But the Lord used my husband to encourage me to start a business with him. I reluctantly agreed, but I wanted to be in agreement with my husband and with what God wanted, so I did it – but I was afraid. By submitting to God's plan instead of choosing to remain in a state of mediocrity, I began to see myself grow as a businesswoman and to overcome my fears.

I began to walk in a higher level of grace, creativity, and tenacity. I would find myself staying up late working on projects and writing business plans for businesses I wanted to create. During that year, my husband and I launched a book production, marketing, and design company. We assisted many pastors, apostles, and five-fold ministry leaders around the world with publishing their books, creating television and radio commercials, flyers, brochures, marketing materials, and so much more.

One of the greatest challenges to the success of your business and being a woman entrepreneur is not your competition but overcoming the temptation of being mediocre. It takes courage to break away from the ordinary and embrace the extraordinary in your life and business, especially when you experience failure. It takes being open to change, even when it is uncomfortable. It takes courage to step out of the comfort of mediocrity, overcome fear, and be the entrepreneur God has called you to be.

Eliminating mediocrity in your life and business requires a focused mindset and a determination to redirect your drive and passion toward your vision and mission. This type of focus is a daily reminder that defeat is not an option and that you are a reward to somebody. A person who chooses to live a life of mediocrity has lost their passion. They have chosen to lie down and accept whatever life's circumstances have brought their way. They no longer want to fight for their destiny, whether in life or as an entrepreneur.

Mediocrity is a thief. Its job is to steal, kill, and destroy your drive, excitement, enthusiasm, and even your potential to increase. Mediocrity is not of God. It's a tool of the devil. Remember what Jesus said in John 10:10, "The thief cometh not but for to steal, and to kill, and to destroy: I am come that they might have life, and that they might have it more abundantly." When you make the decision to become an entrepreneur, you choose to reinvent who you are, step out in faith, and become a risk taker. This is a characteristic that not everyone possesses. You are a cut above, and the enemy knows that. This is why he will try all kinds of tactics to keep you from walking in the fullness of this calling. He will create all kinds of tricks, traps, circumstances, and situations to get you to walk away from your destiny.

If you don't fight against mediocrity, you will willingly give this demonic spirit the right to steal, kill, and destroy the passion, gift, and talent God has given you for such a time as this. Mediocrity will not only rob you of your greatest potential, it will also rob you of the focus needed to succeed. This thief will have you focusing on the wrong things -- your mistakes, limitations, failures, and the success of others. You can't achieve success as an entrepreneur if you remain in a state of mediocrity. Redirect your focus; ask God to forgive you for being fearful, stubborn, and unbelieving. And lastly, come out of agreement with being mediocre and change your way of thinking. Now disrupt the status quo and crush mediocrity under your feet!

TOYA L. GARNER

At the age of twelve years old, I gave my life to Jesus Christ, and as an adult, I committed to serving the Lord as a prophet and teacher. Under these spiritual governing offices, the Lord has anointed me to operate as a spiritual midwife, and with His grace to birth and activate many people into their purpose and destiny. I have also assisted many churches and ministerial leaders with church structure and wise master building. The anointing on my life allows me to scribe, offer strong deliverance, intercessory prayer, interpret dreams, and heal.

My passion for serving and empowering people has allowed me the opportunity to participate on the board of directors for the following non-profit organizations: 713 Community Empowerment Group, Women That Sparkle, and America Serving the Hungry. In addition, I am the CEO of my own company, Toya Garner Enterprises. I have been married to the love of my life, Don Garner, for thirty years, and we have five children and three grandchildren.

If you would like to book a speaking engagement with me, please contact me at booking@toyagarner.com.
WEBSITE: www.toyagarner.com
FACEBOOK: @toyagarnerenterprises
INSTAGRAM: @toyagarner

DISRUPTING THE STATUS QUO

CHAPTER 14

STRENGTH, DETERMINATION & FAITH

BY DR. NATHALIE C. LILAVOIS

My name is Dr. Nathalie C. Lilavois, and I'm from Long Island, New York.

I want to share my entrepreneurial journey with you. Have you ever been hit over and over again before you've had a chance to recover?

In a three-month span, I endured some of the most difficult times of my life. I had fallen into an abyss of sadness, fear, and depression -- a trifecta that could stop anyone in her tracks. The only way I could survive this dark time was with strength, determination, and faith.

And so can you.

November. The call finally came. I held my breath as I answered the phone. This was the boss I could see myself working for, and here she was on the phone with me. I could hardly contain my excitement. Her first words gut-punched me: "I'm sorry, but..." I hardly heard the rest as I realized she had called to tell me I did not get the job. I could barely manage a "Thank you" at the end of the call before I sank down on the sofa and cried. I thought I had prepared well. I thought I aced my interviews. I thought she liked me. I was wrong. I had failed... again. I gathered myself and went to work the next day, deflated, dispirited, disengaged. I repeatedly reviewed everything in my mind, looking for my mistakes, my flaws. What had I done wrong?

December. As time passed, the disappointment faded to the back seat, and I returned to my routine. One day at work, I got another phone call. This one was even worse. It was my sister, crying into the phone that our mom had passed away. I just sat there, alone in my office, staring into space. In a trance, I told my supervisor and barely heard his condolences. I zombied through the rest of my responsibilities in slow motion. Then, I went home to bury my mom. As the eldest, I had the responsibility of orchestrating the funeral arrangements. I cried that Christmas.

January. All the days were the same, and I went through the motions – I wasn't sick, but I was not quite myself, either. I cried at odd times, excusing myself from meetings and abruptly running out. I was embarrassed. I sat there, but I wasn't really there. My thoughts drifted. I was disconnected. I was ineffective, unproductive. My stomach felt a little funny, but there was nothing I could put my finger on. Is this what grief feels like? Something tugged at me to visit my doctor and try to explain this on-again, off-again physical discomfort I was feeling. Was it real? She requested x-rays, and the results prompted her to call a specialist for an immediate appointment. I appreciated the connection, not realizing the reason for the urgency of her call, until my appointment confirmation came... from an oncologist. I had no tears that day.

The specialist couldn't see what was happening behind the dense tissue that had plastered my ovaries to my abdomen after a partial hysterectomy a few years earlier. What was growing there? He was kind and patient while I used the entire box of tissues in his office. Surgery was the only option to remove the scar tissue/ovaries/possible C-word. I signed the papers, prayed for the best, and went to the hospital, preparing myself for the worst.

My mother had survived breast cancer. I could only hope I would be that strong. She and I had a difficult relationship over the years. There were many hurtful memories that she had forgotten. I had not. She had overcome so many challenges that I hadn't fully acknowledged until then. In that moment, I let go of the resentment, and she became my shero. I knew the only way I could survive was to draw on the strength, determination, and faith that had always been the foundation of our family.

Strength. I learned that in the face of the worst adversity, I could persevere. I had raised a child by myself. I had run an award-winning school. I owned my own house and car after bankruptcy. I had done all of this alone, despite the fear that made me doubt my capability and threatened to paralyze me. I knew I could still function and maintain a daily routine. It was not my personal best, but it was the best I had at the time. I was not fully present, but I did what I needed to do, and that was enough.

Determination. I struggled to get out of bed every single day. The snooze button became my best friend. Eventually, I would drag myself out of bed and say out loud, "You can do this," even though I didn't believe it. And I did do it. The days were long and painful, but they ended, and I learned that I won a small victory for making it through each day, and that was enough.

Faith. There were two kinds of faith that served me well -- faith in myself and faith in God. Negative self-talk and affirmations went toe to toe every day in my head. I was mentally exhausted. On a good day, affirmations won and drowned out the negative self-talk. When they didn't, I prayed, and God stepped in to tell me I'd be all right. I asked him, "When?" I learned to enlist His support from the beginning rather than wait until I was falling apart, and that was enough.

These are the lessons I learned that have stayed with me.

There is a well-known quote by Thomas Fuller that says, "It is always darkest before the dawn." You never expect it to apply to your own life. When you feel you just can't cope anymore, find an anchor, a lifeline, a therapist, a friend, a church... whatever. When you do, hang on until the dawn.

Secondly, I firmly believe in the adage "This too shall pass." It is irrefutable that your faith, determination, and strength will see you through the dark times. All you need is that sliver of light coming through the blinds to fight the darkness threatening to consume you. Don't let it.

Each tiny win is one more step in your action plan, and remember, your steps are ordered (Psalm 37:23). Don't let the despair cloud your focus. Keep moving in the direction of your dreams. You may falter, but don't lose hope.

And finally, in the parable, Luke 8:15, true believers bear fruit with perseverance. It is not only your faith, but also your consistent commitment that will see you through the most difficult times and bear harvest in the end. You have to believe in yourself and your purpose. Trust in the divinity within you and claim it as your power. I learned that the everyday struggle was merely a process to move through the challenges. I emerged stronger and steadfast on the other side of the darkness.

So, what happened?

The job I thought I wanted became just a footnote in my journey.

Instead, I found out that I had done things so very right, allowing me to retire early with a pension to maintain a comfortable lifestyle. In doing so, I also circumvented the escalating stress and frustration of working during the pandemic. The door that was shut steered me down a different path that proved to be so much better for me in the long run.

Instead, I started two different businesses that allow me to work on my own terms in education and finance, areas that re-energize my passion. I learn and grow while delivering meaningful content and conversation to help others do the same. I thrive.

Instead, I made peace with my mom by recognizing her love, despite the conflict that divided us. I forgive. I choose how I want to show up for my daughter, every day. I know mom watches over me, and I hope she is proud.

And as for my surgery, I was fortunate enough that the growth was benign. I give thanks. I listen to my body — the restless worry that can rob you of a good night's sleep, the stress-filled knots in your neck and shoulders after back-to-back meetings, the dull ache of another tension headache. All too often, we shrug these aches and pains off and keep going, when in fact, these are signals our body gives us, begging for a time out. I pay attention.

The strength to get through a tragedy, the determination

to keep moving forward, and the faith in my divine purpose allowed me to crush mediocrity and become the **C**onfident, **E**ffective, **O**ptimistic boss of my life and my company.

DR. NATHALIE C. LILAVOIS

Dr. Nathalie C. Lilavois is the CEO and founder of Zahara Crown, Inc., an educational consulting company that provides professional educational support to families, teachers, districts, and organizations with the goal of designing and delivering high quality, positive, engaging learning experiences for students of color. Her mission is to level the playing field by empowering families with the educational and financial information, resources, and tools they need to be successful and build a strong legacy for their future.

Dr. Nat retired after thirty-four years in the educational field as a classroom teacher, principal, district administrator, and college professor. She has received awards recognizing her dedication to education, empowerment, and civic responsibility. Dr. Nat, aka Cpt. Lilavois, is also a veteran of U.S. Army Reserve.

Dr. Nat completed a master's degree from Teachers College, Columbia University, and earned her Doctor of Education degree from Hofstra University. She is a best-selling author whose works include Love Letters to My Girls, Sisters Inspiring Sisters, and

Voices of the 21st Century.

Dr. Nat is the executive producer of TEDxDeerPark, having curated successful TEDx events annually since 2017. She has presented at numerous state and national conferences. Dr. Nat is active in non-profit organizations that reflect her passion and commitment to the development and economic empowerment of women, people of color, and youth, such as Malik Melodies Sisterhood, Inc., Alpha Kappa Alpha Sorority, Inc., and National Coalition of 100 Black Women, Long Island, to name only a few.

To connect with Dr. Nat, visit zaharacrown.com.
WEBSITE: https://www.zaharacrown.com
FACEBOOK: @zahara.crown.inc
INSTAGRAM: @zaharacrown

CHAPTER 15

WOMAN UP, GIRL

BY DESIREE FLEMING

G irl, I am so excited for you! If you could only see what God sees, you would get as excited as I am. This is your "Woman Up" moment, girl. What will you do with it? I'm so thankful God led you to read my chapter. My name is Desiree Fleming, and I am an entrepreneurial woman who has crushed mediocrity in many different areas. I would like to share with you how I crushed being insecure and lazy.

I'm the second oldest of thirteen siblings. From kindergarten through eighth grade, I was often bullied and made to feel as though I didn't fit in. As a kindergartener, I was pulled out of circle time and made to feel different because of how I smelled. Later, I became a teen mom and high-school dropout. I have lived in a shelter and struggled with extreme poverty. Just imagine, I used to go with my mom and siblings to get food out of the garbage can behind the local grocery store! As a teenager, I struggled to financially take care of my son. To tell the truth, back then, I never imagined how my life would turn out. I had no solid plans or goals for my life. Although I had imagined what I could do, I had no drive or definite strategies for how to make anything happen.

Moving out of state with my husband and son when I was twenty-one proved to be a turning point in my life. Actually, it was the second-best decision I made after giving my life to Christ. It was the catalyst that forced me to become a responsible adult and get on my feet financially. With only a ninth-grade education and very limited work experience, I was blessed to have one of my cousins walk me through a crash course of administration to get a job, I was so underqualified for. My confidence began to improve slightly when I enrolled in a local college to get my GED. Because of my fear of succeeding, I struggled at first, but eventually, I completed the course and graduated. Years later, I am back in the very city and state where all those years ago my life began to change. As I sit here in this very space today, without even planning to write my book, I see just how much my life has changed. I am in awe of how God has brought my life full circle.

I remember how I used to struggle with my words when it came to public speaking. I felt so inadequate. I would stumble, rehearsing my words repeatedly, hoping to respond intellectually. That was especially the case when I was around a new group of people who were well-educated and moving ahead in their careers. They never knew the pressure I felt to make sure I said the right thing in the right way so I didn't seem like a dummy. Truth be told, they were an amazing group of individuals who celebrated me for who I was, a woman with a mission to do better and see others accomplish their goals.

Eventually, my husband and I decided to move back home to Illinois. Little by little, the life I once lived there was starting to change in amazing ways. For one thing, I started my own business. Although I had no degree, no training, no understanding of how to run or operate a full-time business, God taught me how to work the numbers, open and close, and create booklets -- every skill that I need to help my business become valuable and needed.

I didn't move back and start my business right away. As I was working, I began having a desire to run my own business. Now, who in the world does that without any type of formal training? I talked it over with my husband. Then I began looking into how to get started. Eventually, I put in my two weeks' notice to my employer. Leaving and starting my business with no money in the bank was truly a faith move. Little did I know that everything I was doing was a stepping-stone for God to catapult me to the next level. For the next ten years, I successfully ran my business. It was profitable and very fulfilling.

And guess what? I didn't even realize all those years that I was an entrepreneur, but I was anointed to do it! During that time of running my business, I started a ministry for women called W.H.O.O.P.S., an acronym for Women Helping Others Overcome Personal Struggles. I hosted multiple workshops, conferences, and mini conferences called "Women Advances," empowering young girls and women to pursue God and His purpose.

Well, it didn't stop there. God began to develop a writer's anointing in me. The first book I wrote was entitled "Where Could I Take My Shame?: The Unprotected Daughter." Many responded with testimonies because of that book, but there was also a lot of criticism about my editing. Whew! Talk about a roller coaster ride! I went from being excited after writing my first book to being ashamed of it. I felt naked. The focus of my story was being overlooked because the book's editing was so poorly done. I had to step back for a while. It reminded me of my days in high school when I didn't feel like I understood the work. I felt like an insecure teenager all over again. I was hurt when a friend told me that I should donate the books. It took me years to realize she wasn't trying to insult me; she was just being honest. She wanted to help me be better and do better since the message of the book was sorely needed and extremely powerful.

I'm not sure exactly when it happened, but one day God lifted that shame and embarrassment and began showing me all the other skill sets that I had, which I had been unaware of. He began positioning me to continue to thrive and evolve into the woman He created me to be. I began to breathe and live again! God spoke to me one day while I was cooking. He said, "You ignite flames in others." I wasn't quite sure it was Him, so I called a friend and asked her what she thought about it. She confirmed that's exactly what I had been doing all along. (Side bar: "Why can't we just accept God's voice when He speaks?") I didn't realize the lives of other people were being changed and shifting for the better as a result of engaging me in conversations, attending conferences I sponsored, or by reading my books. I had no idea

I had been giving them a reason to grow and nurture the gifts God had placed in them.

As God was revealing the gifts and talents in my life, I began to write and publish more books. From there, I began a ten-year run as a playwright, producing multiple stage plays that empowered women, men, and children as the plays were presented in various venues around Chicago. During the tenure of all these productions, I had the amazing opportunity to contract actors and staff. Never in my wildest dreams could I have imagined this accomplishment without God's grace to "Woman Up" and trust Him to shine in me and through me!

Often, we downplay ourselves. This is especially true for us women who have so many insecurities and limitations. We see others doing something, and we quickly make a mental checklist of our skills and talents. We may think something could never be done because we don't have what it takes. We figure, "It's never been done in my family, so how could I do it with little or no resources?" But sister, you are in your "Woman Up, Girl" moment! You have to look beyond those barriers and choose to break through your insecurities. It is your time to give this world something they never would have imagined coming from you!

Your limitations are God's opportunity to catapult you into your next "Woman Up, Girl" moment! It could be your "Woman Up, Girl" in business, your "Woman Up, Girl" move, your "Woman Up, Girl" opportunity, or your "Woman Up, Girl" possibility!

When I started to just lean a little more on God for His will and purpose, He began to reveal more of what He placed in me. Guess what? He's not even done! I am looking forward to my next "Woman Up, Girl" moment. Those moments are my opportunity to advance as a woman, wife, mother, and entrepreneur. Those moments give me the push to "Woman Up, Girl" past any negativity or barriers which oppose my growth. Those moments remind me that I am called to ignite others, like you, to go after all God has deposited in you. Even when you can't see it, God knows what's in you and will reveal it to you little by little.

Now, let me tell you something else. None of this happened in my life because I had the knowledge or training to do any of it. I did not know anything. I started off as a person who never completed anything. Remember, I was a high school dropout. I would start a job and quit it quickly. Then one day I noticed that when I began to associate with others who had higher levels of education than I did, I quickly ruled out mediocrity as an option. When I began to associate myself with business owners, writers, and go-getters, my priorities changed. That was the turning point I reached when my family and I relocated. Everything about my values began to change. That's why I went back to school to get my GED and then on to college to earn my bachelor's degree in urban theology. And now, I am in my fifties and back in school on the dean's list. I don't mind being one of the oldest in my classes. It's okay to keep crushing mediocrity because I don't want it to crush me. That is why I am starting my new movement for 2022: "Woman, Up! Girl!"

There was no way for me to stay insecure and lazy as I surrounded myself with goal-getters who were crushing mediocrity right in my face. The push I received almost thirty years ago now propels me to an even greater level today. If you are ready to go to the next level, you have to begin by changing the circle of people you associate with. There is no other way to do it. I'm not saying to excommunicate your friends. I'm just setting a challenge before you. If you want to see something different, experience something different, then you will have to do something different. Trust me, it will be uncomfortable in the beginning, but if you are to uncover all God has invested in you, you have to be around those who can help you "Woman Up, Girl!"

DESIREE FLEMING

Desiree Fleming is an entrepreneur, wife, mother, author, playwright, motivational strategist, speaker and evangelist.

Known as Lady Des and Coach Des, Desiree possesses a powerful and uplifting voice she uses to deliver inspiration, empowerment, and motivation to women, men, and teens.

Desiree was a teen mom and high school dropout, but has, by God's grace, overcome a life of poverty and the mindset that accompanies such struggle. Desiree is transparent about the strife she faced growing up. She also shares what it was like growing up in a home where her mother experienced domestic abuse. Desiree saw her mother nearly killed by her stepfather, and when Desiree was a teen, she herself was in a domestic violent relationship that she broke free from.

Over the past twenty years, Desiree has dominated the entrepreneur business world of stage play productions, book publishing, motivational speaking, writers' coaching, personal and development coaching, igniting flames in others to plan, pursue, and produce. The heart of her ministry and mission is to ignite flames in others.

Desiree and her community extension feed families for Thanksgiving, provide blankets for the homeless, and provide care packs and backpacks for schoolchildren.

Desiree travels extensively, sharing words of inspiration to empower children, teens, and women. In addition, she coaches individuals from homemakers to medical doctors to help them with writing, strategizing, planning, empowerment, and motivation. She challenges her audience to never give up, even if others don't believe in them.

Desiree's bold and beautiful presence graces the stage with pure resilience and transparency. Her clarion call is to always find the "I" in win.

Contact information:
WEBSITE: www.coachdestalks.com
EMAIL: coachdestalks@gmail.com
FACEBOOK: CoachDes Talks
INSTAGRAM: Coach Des Talks

DISRUPTING THE STATUS QUO

CHAPTER 16

LIFE'S PRISONS CAN'T HOLD ME

BY RAMONA ROGERS

"Above all, be the heroine of your life, not the victim"
-NORA EPHRON

My name is Ramona Rogers, and I'm from Tulsa, Oklahoma. I am an entrepreneurial woman who has crushed mediocrity. I want to share with you my story.

Life's prisons are no match for the human will to survive. Have you ever felt totally invisible, helpless, like you have been imprisoned with no way to escape?

As a four-year-old I felt like a death sentence was placed on my life because of the negative words of others. Between the ages of four and eight, I was repeatedly told that I was dumb. My sense of self was bound, handcuffed, shackled, and left for dead. Nobody likes a dummy, I had concluded. Since I was incapable of learning, I felt like I was unworthy of love. The prison of pain eventually turned to my mastering the art of being invisible in plain sight. Separating my inner self from my physical self was my way of coping with and maneuvering in life.

At the age of nineteen, I found myself in prison yet again and feeling helpless. I was imprisoned by a boy who displayed his misguided love for me with words and deeds that were mentally, emotionally, and physically abusive. His constant threat to end my life and the lives of my family members if I ever left him kept me living in a prison of fear for six years.

I often wondered why I had to endure such pain and how much more could I take.

I know what it's like to feel unworthy.

During various seasons of my life, I felt like I was imprisoned either mentally or emotionally. From the time I was young, my mind was imprisoned with the stigma of incompetence, therefore; my outlook on life was like living in an abyss of mediocrity. I had low to no standards, and my highest ambition was to be a domestic goddess. This was something that I learned from watching my mother run her household of eight children with the deftness of a military sergeant. With no high school diploma, but a gift for discipline, structure, organization, and management, I mimicked the domestic traits of my mother. My imprisoned mind forbid achievement in any other arena. I concluded that honing my domestic skills would keep me employed as a blue-collar worker for the rest of my life.

I was seeking only to exist in life because I had no point of reference from which to gauge the difference between actually living life and just existing in life. When you believe your possibilities are limited, you play it small. I became a victim to thinking that a life of mediocrity was just what I was to expect. I believed that life's circumstances were happenstance, and I had to play the hand that life dealt me. My imprisoned mind caused me to conform to mediocrity, and it forced me to be confined to limited thoughts that led to limited actions.

I always thought the so-called good life was meant for other people, particularly those who were not people of color. The environments and experiences available to me seemed to offer only struggle, lack, and never enough, which further supported my restricted belief about who I was and my place in the world.

After the birth of my second daughter, I was diagnosed with a severe case of postpartum depression, and that made me feel like I was in prison all over again. Postpartum depression is a chemical imbalance that doesn't allow one to function like one normally would. It causes feelings of helplessness and hopelessness. Because of my having those feelings, my daughters had to be removed from my home in order to keep them safe. The feelings of helplessness and hopelessness were too familiar. I had felt this way most of my life. Life felt like a mundane cycle of moving the proverbial needle three steps forward, then losing ground and being pushed four steps back. This depression was just life's happenstance, and I just had to deal with it as best as I could, as always.

It wasn't until the chemicals in my brain achieved balance and my daughters were returned to my home that life took a turn in a different direction. Once I saw my girls' faces, I had an overwhelming epiphany that changed the trajectory of my life. In that moment I decided that my daughters would not live a life of mediocrity and limits like I had. I knew that they would learn most of who they were to become by watching me, just like I had learned from my mother. I decided that I loved myself and my daughters enough to muster up the courage to fight for my existence and escape the prisons of life that had held me captive for far too long.

I had to change my thinking and accept the fact that I was worthy to be loved and to live a life of abundance. I had to stop accepting the lies and negative labels that I had allowed to define me. I had to change the limiting beliefs about who I was and the treasures that I embodied.

I had to ask myself:

When was I going to accept the fact that I was born to be better?

When was I going to accept the fact that I deserve better?

When was I going to take the necessary actions to make myself better?

I had to embark on a journey of self-discovery to learn who I was. There were so many questions about my identity. What were my dreams, gifts, talents, strengths, and weaknesses? These questions began to help me gain insight about what I wanted to become and how I wanted my life to look. I saw where I wanted to go, and I created a strategy that would allow me to break the chains that had bound my mind. I would gain new knowledge and new information. This was the key that would help me unlock a new outlook on life. To change myself from the inside out, I immersed myself into personal development.

I started reading self-help books and listening to motivational speakers. They all advocated following your dreams and doing the things that brought you joy and that brought out the best in you.

The more I learned, the more I was able to embrace the many possibilities that life had to offer. I was not only gaining knowledge and developing my skills, but I was also able to apply my new knowledge, which allowed me to transform my mind from having a limited outlook to understanding that possibilities are endless.

One of the most disturbing facts I learned was that there are so many layers to life, and my experience was not an isolated one. In fact, there are a great number of adults who are not equipped with the tools needed to achieve and maneuver in life.

I began researching successful people. I wanted to know the secrets to success. What I learned is that there are no secrets to success. There are only systems to success.

With this new understanding, I begin crafting success systems that would change the outlooks and outcomes of the Ramonas of the world. Through this process I started believing in myself and my abilities. I had to develop my skills, gifts, talents and then implement the systems and methods that would help me to achieve my goals and dreams.

The challenge then became my willingness to get out of the comfort zone of my subconscious mind. The comfort zone felt like a prison that was preventing me from desiring any type of elevation or longing for achievement. It sought to constantly revert me to the familiar instead of pursuing the uncertainty of the unknown. My comfort zone was fighting to keep me in the prison of mediocrity.

The systems I created challenge the status quo and the mindset and provide intentionality and alignment that allows the dream seeker to one day live their dream. I've learned that if you aren't challenged in life, you won't change your life.

I am a three-time published author, a personal development coach, a motivational speaker, trainer, and facilitator. My purpose in life is to empower and encourage the masses to think differently about who they are and their abilities, to dream their biggest dreams and create their blueprints for success -- to live their lives by design.

RAMONA ROGERS

Ramona Rogers has been an entrepreneur for over twenty years. She is a three-time author, personal development coach, motivational speaker, and facilitator. Her childhood experiences caused her to have limited beliefs about herself and the possibilities of life. Situations and circumstances led her to fight for her existence and for her daughters' future. The pains she endured as a child became what drives her passion today. She entered early childhood education, and she owned and operated related businesses for more than fifteen years. During those years she coached employees, parents, and students on how to show up at their best. She was doing this on a regular basis and became both a certified life coach and certified executive coach. While coaching, she continued to search for better ways to empower people to change their mindsets about who they were and the treasures that they embodied. Helping others discover their potential for greatness became her focus. She learned that the best way for people to elevate themselves is to incorporate systems into their lives. Her gifts to the world are her programs,

Blueprint for Success and Gr8ness in the Making, along with the many books she has written. Ramona is passionate about helping others elevate themselves and reach their potential for greatness. She is on a mission to make sure the masses are equipped with the tools and knowledge to continuously become the best version of themselves.

Connect with Ramona:
www.ramonarogers.com
EMAIL: ramona@ramonarogers.com
*INSTAGRAM: ramona_rogers_*
FACEBOOK: Ramona Rogers
LINKEDIN: Ramona Rogers

CHAPTER 17

I Took One for the Team

BY TIA MONET SINGLETON

My name is Tia Monet Singleton, and I am from Chicago, Illinois. I am an entrepreneurial woman who has crushed mediocrity, and I want to share my story. I am resilient; mental illness does not define me.

Nothing happens without a cause. All events, actions and circumstances have an origin. Sometimes in the midst of a chaotic situation, it is difficult to identify the origin, but, if we look really closely and investigate, we will notice what is not apparent. Looking over my life, I have many times asked why -- not so much why me – just why. What is behind all this chaos, bad decisions, sickness, disappointment, and anger? There has to be a reason. I refuse to believe that I am cursed, because I understand what the scriptures say. However, all of *this* came from somewhere; there has to be a starting point. Looking back, I have discovered that there have always been little clues that I missed or ignored. They were left like breadcrumbs leading me to where I need to be and assisting me through the journey to my destination. Some say we should enjoy the journey, but I don't know that I necessarily believe that. I believe we arrive at a place where there are lessons learned, and we experience what Oprah describes as an "aha moment." My life in particular has been what could be defined as chaotic or even in the most compassionate terms, crazy. Then it is no surprise where my life has landed. Now, instead of asking why I simply lovingly embrace myself and work through whatever I am facing. I call it "embracing my crazy," because life has conditioned me to do so, to accept what has been revealed.

I got lost in Omaha, Nebraska. Being lost is not crazy at all, because people get lost every day. It could happen to anyone,

101

but not when you are eleven years old and traveling from San Francisco, California, to Chicago, Illinois, *alone*. That's right. I was traveling by myself on the Greyhound bus for three days. My mother was struggling to take care of me and sent me to live with my grandmother. When I got to Nebraska, we had to get off the bus for a break, and I went into the station to use the bathroom and get something to eat. Many of the details are a blur, but somehow, I lost my purse and all its contents, including money, a note from my mother, and my bus tickets. I must have been sleepy, because when I realized what happened, it seemed as if the room was spinning. I couldn't find my possessions anywhere. My bus was about to leave me, and I had no boarding ticket. The driver didn't know me. I had gotten used to people shaking their heads when they saw me. Can you say trauma? I never cried so hard. I have never been so scared. I called my mother collect from a pay phone in the station, as you can imagine, hysterical. I could barely speak and probably sounded like I was screaming. I can't even remember the conversation, but just then someone tapped me on the shoulder. They pointed to the service desk where a man dressed in a Greyhound uniform was standing. I hung up with my mother, and while trying to catch my breath and still crying, I went over to the man. He handed me my purse. I was able to complete my journey. That is just one incident of many that has led me to one conclusion. Apparently crazy runs in my family. To know is half the battle.

Growing up in the church, I learned very quickly that transparency is a no-no, especially if it relates to mental illness. Mental illness is treated as a totally separate organism from any other infirmity or disease. Although the head (brain and central nervous system) is one of the most vital operating systems in the body, the church treats illness of this system with a polarized reaction. The person suffering is either demon possessed, or nothing is wrong with them at all, because it's all an act. Reaction is either extreme or nothing. In most cases the latter is the reaction. Most people in church leadership positions have no idea how to handle a person suffering with mental illness. Be clear, mental illness is a generic description for a wide range of illnesses affecting the brain. For me in particular, before I even knew I was affected, I suffered from depression, anxiety, and panic attacks -- sometimes all at once. Can you imagine what it feels like to be "crazy" and not know it? I lovingly look back at the angry outbursts, uncontrollable crying, irresponsible spending, and intense fear. It felt like I was in the world alone, because to tell someone is to be dismissed, ostracized, or exposed. So, I learned to bury my feelings and experiences until they came to a head -- a dangerous, almost deadly head.

In February 2009, just after I turned forty, I had a mental breakdown. As Charles Dickens wrote, "It was the best of times, and it was the worst of times." I hadn't slept longer than two hours a day for about six weeks. During that time, I worked nights at a factory and was up all night and up all day. I could feel myself slipping, but I didn't know what to do about it. One night I started thinking about my mom, grandmother, and aunt, all of whom had died in about an eight-month time frame. My whole support system was gone in a year and a half. There was no time to grieve; I had to work and take care of seven children. I was so sad and depressed and going through the motions. No one knew that I was at the brink of a suicidal breakdown. It all made perfect sense at that moment. People often ask, "How could they do that?" To answer the question, no rational person would. But when your mind snaps, your irrational thoughts make perfect sense. One night, about 3 a.m., I was not only suicidal, I was also homicidal, because my mind said to kill the children also, so they wouldn't have to find my dead body. I woke my daughter Britney up. I was screaming, because in me there was still God saying "No, you will not kill yourself or the children." There was an unimaginable war going on inside me. I told Britney my plans and was met with a look of fear and calm. She sat me down, removed the knives (I don't remember getting them), and began to call for help. I was still crying, screaming, and wrestling with the yes-and-no battle going on in my head.

It seemed for a while that yes was winning, but help came. I don't remember if I arrived at the hospital by ambulance, police, or what means, I just remember being there. By that morning I watched my son and best friend, who had signed me into the psych ward, wave goodbye as large steel doors slowly shut behind me. I am grateful for what I believe was five days of intense therapy. I found myself during that time away from all that was familiar. I learned what triggers me, and I learned that even Christians experience mental illness.

It is safe to say that most people would be embarrassed to share such an unflattering account of two very painful events. However, in my humble opinion, I believe one of the first actions in the movement toward crushing mediocrity is transparency. To say with certainty that the status quo will be disrupted in our lives, we must embrace our past and accept our today, thereby honestly equipping ourselves to face the future. Transparency does not only benefit the one telling the story, it also offers liberty for another person held hostage by the painful memories to tell theirs. Make no mistake -- life will not always offer mountain-top victories. More times than not it will bring valley defeats, and both are necessary for growth and development. It is memories of the moments of defeat that give me the compassion to champion the plight of the underdog, especially when it concerns people suffering with mental illness. I am partial to the Black female Christian, because they each have a difficult time overcoming the stigma attached to mental illness. I will not be silent until there are honest conversations and notable changes. Disrupting (to destroy the structure of) the status quo starts with being honest with yourself, listening to others, and taking immediate action that directly changes our paths of destruction. I will take one for the team.

Tia Monet Singleton

Tia M. Singleton hails from Chicago, Illinois, and is an international powerhouse preacher and teacher of the Word of God. She serves as a skilled assessor at Matthew House Inc., which is indicative of a life of serving the community and her country. Tia is a United States Army veteran and a former Chicago police officer. She is a graduate of Ferris State and Destiny Christian universities. She deems motherhood her greatest accomplishment and has raised eight children. Tia is an entrepreneur, business owner, and a sought-after conference speaker. She is a champion for the underdog and a woman who never limits her possibilities. She believes in keeping one's eyes and ears open, because neither have seen nor heard what God has in store.

FACEBOOK & INSTAGRAM: @tia.singleton.94

DISRUPTING THE STATUS QUO

CHAPTER 18

A LEAP OF FAITH

BY CHERYL BOONE

I'm Cheryl Boone, and I reside In Chicago, Illinois. I am an entrepreneurial woman who crushed mediocrity and disrupted the status quo by no longer listening to the voices that would tell me I'm not good enough. I broke out of my prison of mediocrity and dared to do what I didn't think I could. Come go with me as I lead you down my journey.

My story starts with a prayer walk. I walk in the park around my house. I call it the walking park, because it seems like everyone in the neighborhood has a scheduled time to walk in the park. As I was walking one beautiful summer day, I was talking with God, out in the fresh air, wind blowing on my face. I was just praying, and I heard God whisper, in that still, small voice: "Write a book of poetry about your family, ministry, and Me."

I said, "Write a book? I'm not an author," and God said it again: "Write a book of poetry."

I said, "Okay, God," but you best believe when I said yes to God, I was afraid. I didn't know where to start or even what to do. I sometimes wanted to take back the yes. I didn't see myself as He sees me. The thoughts and questions that started flooding my mind haunted me. Who would listen to me? What do I have to say that can help someone else? The battle in the mind is real, and sometimes it will talk me right out of the will of God.

I had been writing songs and poems for years, but I never considered myself an author. The things I was writing were just because God was giving me new songs from an open heaven. I consider myself a psalmist, a songwriter, like David. I would hear music with the lyrics. I didn't even understand the gift I had. Year ago, I sang with the praise and worship team, and God was giving us so many new songs, we didn't even have to sing music from a known artist. Whenever my co-pastor would need a poem for a special event, she would come to me and ask me to write a poem for the occasion, and as sure as she would ask, God would give the words to me. I said she had a way of pulling on the anointing in my life. With all that writing I was doing, still I didn't consider myself an author, and when God said to write a book, I was still unsure.

No one really saw the things I wrote -- a poem here and there in the church or a song the praise and worship team would sing. My writings never went past the four walls of the church. Only a few people knew that I had a catalog full of songs. I would write them and put them into a notebook. But, this time God wanted me to write something that the whole world would see! Can you imagine all that was going on in my head? Will people judge my every word? What if what I write doesn't sound right? What if it sounds good only to me? But I knew if the Lord was asking me to do this, surely He would equip me, so I had to trust God and just leap.

I was afraid to connect with people I didn't know. I was concerned that someone would steal my music. Countless times, I wanted to reach out for help from accomplished people in the music industry, and my fears of rejection stopped me. I was held captive in my thoughts and actions, and they paralyzed me from moving forward and connecting with my purpose. Nevertheless, I declared to myself that what transpired with my music would not take place with my books. Unlike my music, I didn't need a minstrel, or singers, or drummers or horn players. All I needed to do was take the leap.

I didn't know what I was doing, had no connections or resources. I felt all alone, hopeless sometimes, with a gift and a talent that I know God had given me, but I felt unseen, unnoticed, almost invisible, and I felt like everything I had to do, I had to figure out on my own. I was determined to crush mediocrity and rise up to that place that God was calling me to, that place He needed me to be in, so I just took the leap and stepped out and reached out to someone I could trust. That person introduced me to their resources, and the journey began. I put my faith in action this time, moved toward my next step, and as I did, doors began to open, and favor began to be given. Following the lead of the Lord will take you somewhere; it will take you to places that you've never been and put you before great men and women of God who can help you accomplish the thing he asks you to do, so you just have to do it, even if you have to do it afraid, break out of the prison of mediocrity, and disturb the status quo.

The new year came. We were in 2020, the year of perfect vision, and all I knew is I wanted to see what God wanted me to see. Lo and behold, Covid-19 hit, and the whole world began to shut down. We were in a pandemic, and everybody was shut up in their homes with no way out, fear running rampant, people dying by the thousands, and everyone was afraid.

In that time and in that season of desperation, God started speaking. He said, "Build me an altar and come before me in worship and pray, and I will meet you."

I would go to my prayer room, put on some worship music and pray, then I would sit in silence, and the Lord began to give me the words to start my book of prophetic poetry. Not only did he give me one book, as soon as I finished one, He began to speak about a second book. I couldn't believe it. I was actually writing heartfelt prophetic poetry about my family, naming and titling short prophetic poetry stories about all those who had gone before me and made their transition to glory. Even as I wrote, the Lord said, "Your stories about your family will remind others about their loved ones who are gone, and it will bring back sweet memories of times gone by."

I published my first book in June 2020 and have finished my second one. It's at the publisher now. I have inspirational apparel that came from my book, Poems From The Heart, which inspires people to be who God called them to be. This is all because I decided to step out of the prison of mediocrity and disrupt the status quo.

That's how I got started on this journey as an author and

entrepreneur. I'm here to encourage you. I believe everyone has a story waiting to be told. You have a business in you, so I want to say to you: Listen to that voice within that keeps telling you you were born to win, and when you get discouraged and can't see your way out, when you're afraid and full of doubt, hold on to your dreams with all your heart and don't let go, because dreams come true for those who continue to pursue. No matter how long it takes, no matter what disappointment life makes, no matter how many rejections you face, don't give up on yourself. Let your rejections help you grow and be strong. Continue to hold on.

We all hear the voice; we just don't respond. There is something in all of us pushing and driving us to fulfill that call. You just have to listen and respond. Believe me, I'm still learning to walk in what I hear. Believe in yourself and start the work that is burning inside you -- you know, that thing that keeps nagging at you, that keeps coming up year after year that you keep saying you're going to do -- you know, that thing. If you have to do it afraid, do it afraid, until your faith is bigger than your fears. Come on, do what you think is impossible; do what you think is unbelievable; do what they say you can't do, and do what God said you can! Disrupt the status quo... all it takes is a leap of faith.

CHERYL BOONE

Cheryl Boone resides in Chicago, Illinois. She has been married for thirty-five years to her loving husband, Kenneth Boone. They have three children and three grandchildren.

Cheryl Boone is a psalmist and a songwriter, entrepreneur, and author. Her first book, "Poems From The Heart," which was birthed through an encounter with God, was featured in Today's Purposed Woman Magazine. She has been writing songs and prophetic poetry for more than a decade. As a veteran of the United States Armed Forces and former retiree from corporate America, Cheryl considers herself a finisher. Everything in her life is intertwined with dedication and longevity.

As founder and CEO of I Write A Song Ministries, Cheryl endeavors to create a safe space for other artists like herself, to produce a divine and fresh sound to impact the kingdom. Her clothing line, Poems From the Heart, inspires those to align with God to produce fruit of the spirit.

As head elder of administration, board member, psalmist and servant, she serves diligently at the Master's Touch Church, a place of faith, courage, and strength and an oasis where leaders find rest.

www.poemsfromtheheart.shop
poemsfromtheheart.shop@gmail.com
FACEBOOK: @Cheryl Boone
INSTAGRAM: @cheryl.boone.758

DISRUPTING THE STATUS QUO

CHAPTER 19

Identity:
Taking the ME Out
of Mediocrity

BY ROCKKEYA GASTON

A strong sense of who you are will empower you to disrupt the status quo and take the me out of mediocrity. ~ Rockkeya Gaston

Who am I? This question was asked as a reflective writing assignment presented to me in elementary school. As I sat at my desk immersed in the childlike and grandeur description of myself, I uttered these words: I am a girl; I am kind; I am beautiful; I am smart, and I am a child of God. To my eight-year-old self, the I Am's seemed innocent and carefree. But I later learned that in between those whimsical affirmations of I Am's that I affectionately held on to and that carried me into adulthood stood a woman who had grown to struggle with her identity. I am not sure when the struggle began, but the planted seeds of labels, expectations, failures, darts thrown, my striving to always being the "good girl" and the greatest seed of all – *fear* -- had somehow joined forces and covered me like a tattoo. Under it all, though, was a blueprint that I had only tapped into and not fully discovered. I evolved over time and learned to embrace a unique aspect: my identity.

Merriam-Webster defines *identity* as the distinguishing character or personality of an individual. It is what separates us from the other 7 billion (more or less) humans in the world, the part of us that makes us unique. Years later, when I asked myself who I was, I struggled to answer. Take a moment right now and ask yourself, "Who am I?" How did it feel asking? There is no one who knows you better than you. But it *seems* as if others

113

can answer the question more accurately. We know who we are, but we either downplay, embellish, or are so buried in the rubble that we find it too challenging to define.

My struggle with identity came from defining myself by what I did not have or did not see and what I knew about myself. I measured my identity not by what I had accomplished but by my lack of accomplishments. For every accomplishment I made, lack of accomplishment would remind me otherwise, which determined my value as a human being and caused me to measure myself against others. Defining ourselves by the jobs we hold, the roles we execute, and the social affiliations we are attached to compels us to seek external validation for lack of internal identification.

I found myself bombarded with trying to compile years of unachieved goals, accomplishments, and success into a limited time frame, only to spiral into a perpetual cycle of disappointment and feeling overwhelmed. I simply tried too hard to be me when I did not know who being me was. Meanwhile, others defined me by what they thought I had, what they saw or perceived but did not know.

When You Know Who You Are, *Believe It*!

Not knowing who you are or what your purpose is can keep you stuck in a place where mediocrity thrives, and it can become the theme for our lives.

I would often hear people say, "I'm going to find myself." What are we looking for when we go in search of ourselves? What do we discover? I discovered that we are a process; we change much over time; we activate the power within. Everything I needed did not have to be found; it just had to be developed, because it was already within. The blueprint was already there. Every cycle of life changes our identity but not our blueprint. I am not the same person I was twenty years ago or even one year ago because I am always evolving. We are more than our traits, upbringing, situations, mishaps, and setbacks. Our identity comes when we find a point of reference within ourselves that will continue to propel us to do greater, bring change, and make an impact. It is done authentically, void of competition or the need to be relevant. It is done because others around us are propelled to do greater because of our actions.

This is what I call being an entrepreneur in a non-traditional way. I don't have a multi-million-dollar business, but by faith, grace, humility, and love, I have knowingly and unknowingly changed lives around me and benefited from those jewels by creating or attracting more opportunities. Being a part of this amazing project is an example of that. I am confident that the hand of God is going to move immensely in this anthology project. Our faith, thoughts, and actions expand us, enlarge our territory. This is the mind of entrepreneurship. This is the mind of excellence, which means mediocrity has no place; it must be crushed.

My love for writing has also allowed me to discover my identity to some degree because writing evokes reflection, and reflection evokes direction. In reflecting, new ideas are discovered, revelations are released, and order is restored. Much of my writing led to meditation, placing me in direct communion with God. That's powerful because I never thought that the very gift from God -- writing -- would ultimately draw me closer to Him, bestow blessings upon me, and position me to meet people who have paved the way for me and have opened doors I never imagined. I always say, "When you find yourself in that good place, stay there, and when you know who you are, believe it."

Disrupting the Status Quo

Disrupt is a powerful word. It sounds aggressive, and it is. But disruption can be rewarding. We are talking about disrupting the status quo. You know -- the same ol', same ol'. But we can disrupt that mindset by breaking barriers and making what former Civil Rights Leader John Lewis called "good trouble." So, one of the barriers I broke was pretending. I was a great pretender. I pretended to be happy, pretended to agree, pretended that it was okay when it wasn't -- you get the picture. I was merely going through the motions. I displaced and misunderstood humility. It was not okay to allow actions and behaviors that needed attention and for correction to go unnoticed.

I began realizing that not only was I growing exhausted from pretending, but I was also getting older. I had seen the same mentality in women who were educated, iconic, great mothers, mentors, and best-selling authors. So, I started paying attention to women near and far who defined what disrupting the status quo looked like. Some I only heard of or read about; others I knew personally. For the sake of honor and credibility, I must say my mentor and spiritual mom, Apostle Sanja Rickette Stinson, is one of those women. Even her silence is impactful. This is an example of when power meets potential. So, when the mantle is thrown, will you pick it up or leave it there? Can you be trusted with the *moment*?

I am forever grateful to be a combined effort of many great women. Disrupting the status quo was not achieved by a single event; there were events over time that one day shook me and said, "That's enough." I am no longer an onlooker but an active participant in my *own* life. That's what I call identity ownership. I had joined the *me* team by plucking the *me* out of mediocrity in a meaningful and healthy way. Today, I celebrate my voice, my heart, and my mind without guilt nor apologies. My identity is expressed in many facets. There are days you will hear me bringing the *word*, and other days you will be surprised to hear me singing the lyrics to Katy Perry's *Roar*! This is my dedication song for disrupting the status quo and crushing mediocrity. I am continually seeking my heavenly Father in this journey.

So, I leave you with this: there is only one you. Every day you will get closer to yourself through self-examination, reflection, and exploration. There will be times you will have challenges, but don't become defined by them. Examine your speech because it reflects your heart. Examine your feelings and meditate on how to control them. Use your voice on paper and out loud. Look in the mirror and explore yourself. That's your outer identity. Then close your eyes and look inside yourself. Be cognizant of what you see. When I do this, I see my inner identity, my blueprint. I also see the works of God through Psalm 139:13-14:

For you created my innermost being; you knit me together in my mother's womb. 14 I praise you because I am fearfully and wonderfully made. Wow! How powerfully refreshing. Now, that's crushing mediocrity and disrupting the status quo.

LADY ROCKKEYA GASTON

Lady Rockkeya Gaston is a leader and servant clothed with strength and dignity. Affectionately referred to as the "Quiet Spirit," she is a powerful force in the ministry. She is a member of True Love Christian Church, where she labors diligently beside her husband, Pastor Michael A. Gaston, Sr. She serves as a youth Sunday School teacher, overseer of "Women of Praise" dance ministry and is a Bible teacher. She is a co-teacher of diverse learners at Chicago Public Schools. She is also a member of Women on the Frontline International, founded by Apostle Dr. Sanja Rickette Stinson.

She is a mother of three adult children and grandmother of twins, whom she affectionately calls her two heartbeats. She is expanding her education in human services leadership and administration, advocating for children. She is a contributing author to three power-packed books and is working on her own manuscript with an anticipated release Summer of 2022.

The goal of her story on identity is to inspire and impact women who are on the path to finding their rhythm. She wants to inspire women who seeking to "take the me out of mediocrity" through self-examination, reflection, and exploration. Her motto is "When you find yourself in that good place, stay there, and when you know who you are, believe it." To God be the glory!

rockkeya-warren@att.net
www.truelovecc.org
FACEBOOK: @SerenityRock

CHAPTER 20

REALLY?
THAT'S WHAT YOU THOUGHT?

BY CHRISTINE BOWEN

My name is Christine Bowen, and I am from Houston, Texas. I am a female authorpreneur who has crushed mediocrity through overcoming generational cycles. At age thirteen I overheard my aunts talking about me. They said that I would never amount to anything and that I would get pregnant before I finished high school. I could not believe that the people who supposedly loved me so much could hurt me so much. My aunts were mocking me, laughing at me. I could not believe what I was hearing. It felt as if I'd never known these people. I was crushed; I wanted to run and hide, but I could not move. I was forced to listen as they judged me without knowing me – making assumptions based on the history of a mother who abandoned me after birth and a father who was just a lover. He was a lover, a heavy drinker, gambler, and womanizer who was never meant to be a father or a husband.

From that day forward I vowed to prove them wrong. I wanted to ask them, "Really? That's what you thought?" They are no longer with us today, but if they were, I would now thank them. Had I not overheard their painful words, I would not have become angry enough to fight for a better life. I wiped away the tears, lifted my head, and began to walk toward destiny, living with purpose, shattering the old clichés of African American women growing up in the 'hood without a father, being barefoot and pregnant, living on government assistance, and wanting no better. The word "no" does not fit me, nor does it stop me. Working in corporate America taught me that for every no, there is a yes. You cannot give up in the process of winning. Keep moving until you get that yes, and give God praise

119

through the process.

One of the hardest things to do is to continue moving forward when the world seems to be against you. I cannot speak for anyone else, but if your family does not have your back, then who else can you depend on or count on when you are feeling low, feeling as though there is no hope, feeling left out, feeling invisible to those who say they love you? I was an impressionable little girl. I knew that I was different, but I never knew that I would one day learn that people I sat at the dinner table with, spent the night with, and whose children – my cousins – I played with would think so little of me. I shared feelings, emotions, good times, and tough times with them and never knew until the day I overheard them that I was the target of their disdain. I was secretly being ridiculed and laughed at, but what they did not know was that deep down inside me lived a fighter, an overcomer who never runs from adversity but meets it head on. I took that opportunity and all the hurt, pain, and disappointment that came with it to catapult me into my destiny. You will never know what is inside you until you have to fight your way through to see the victory.

I stopped playing around and took my education seriously. I took note of all that my aunts said and started analyzing and restructuring my life. During my senior year in high school, I applied for a radiology technician program offered by a hospital in Kansas City, Kansas. At first, I felt intimidated and fearful because I was attending a school that had about five hundred students, but only fifty of them were African American. Of the twenty applications submitted, the hospital accepted only five. About two weeks after I had submitted my application, I received a call to come in for an interview. When I walked in, I remember seeing some of my classmates who had made my life a living hell.

During the interview, I had to answer a few questions. The one question that stood out to me was "Why should you be accepted into this program?" I was so nervous that it felt as though I could not speak. I kept hearing my aunts' negative

120

words. I remember taking a deep breath and opening my mouth. I said, "Because I care." I described what was in my heart and explained why I was the right person for the program. When I left the interview, I felt as though I could have done better. Did I forget to say some things that could have helped me? I heard that others there believed that I would not be accepted. They laughed at me and said I'd wasted my time. A week later, though, I learned that I was one of the five who had been accepted into the radiology technician program. I was overjoyed. I told my mother the good news and that I needed to buy scrubs and nursing shoes and pay a $200 fee. But she did not have the money to help me. My heart sank; here I was in my senior year of high school being accepted into a two-year program that would take me into a career in the medical field, and $200 was holding me back. However, I was determined, so I started working at McDonald's, doing anything and everything I could do to pay the fee and get my uniforms. Still, it did not happen. Instead, something happened that would shake my very foundation -- and that was the death of the man I called Dad.

I was in a place of loss and deep pain. I was having to deal with all these emotions while replaying the words spoken over my life when I was thirteen. "She'll never amount to anything." It seemed that no matter how hard I tried, I just could not break through. I had to shift my focus to helping my mother, who was now a widow. She did not make much money as a housekeeper, and government assistance was not enough, so I had to work to help support the home. As time passed, the opportunity for me to take some classes in community college opened, and I started school. I began to discover more about me and what I really desired and loved. I had grabbed at an opportunity with the hospital as a way out, but that was not the desire that God had for me. Sometimes we settle for what we think we need instead of living with purpose to seek the things that give us fulfillment and joy. Stepping out in faith and applying for that program helped me to know that I would, I could, and I did. I was accepted into the program, so I won! I did not just sit in the status quo or mediocrity of generational cycles. I broke free through perseverance and resilience.

This experience helped me to have no fear through the journey of life. At the age of twenty-nine, I applied to the United States Navy. I took what I thought was the ASVAB for the enlisted, but the chief who gave me the test had given me an officer's exam. The Navy informed me that I passed and almost made it as a co-pilot to fly an F-16 fighter jet, but I was too old. So, the Navy classified my position under intelligence. Again, something happened that I never saw coming. A jealous husband left me in Norfolk, Virginia, with the children so that I could not report for duty. Nevertheless, that did not stop me. I did not make it into the Navy, but I am a college graduate completing my doctoral degree; I am a three-time author, co-pastor, and CEO of Real Talk Just 4 Women and Living on Purpose broadcast. Do not let the afflictions of life stop you from fulfilling your purpose and destiny. You must be willing to disrupt the status quo. Break out of your shell of mediocrity and step out into the deep. So many of you have heard the same words that I have and more. Just take a moment and say to yourself, "Really? That's what you thought?" One way to cancel a lie is to face it head on. Whenever you think that you cannot make it or that things might not work out the way that you planned, stand in front of the mirror, take a hard look at yourself, and say, "Really? That's what you think?" Fight the lie that lives inside you and keeps you from fulfilling your goals, dreams, and desires. My two aunts can't see my success, but through forgiveness I can see that they were used to light the fire to ignite the overcomer in me to crush mediocrity. You do not have to be like anyone else. Be you! Just being you crushes the mediocrity that keeps you stagnant.

CHRISTINE BOWEN

Prophetess Christine Bowen is co-pastor alongside her husband at Immanuel Temple of Praise Ministries, International, in Houston, Texas. She is an author, Christian counselor, CEO/ founder of Real Talk Just 4 Women and Living on Purpose A.K.A. (Asserting Kingdom Authority) broadcast on BGKNETWORK. ORG. She is an advocate for those who do not have a voice, speaking out for injustice against children and for mental health awareness in the community while helping others to find resources to meet their needs. She has dedicated her life to empower, encourage, and motivate women to live past their past through transparency by sharing their testimonies of recovery, sexual and physical abuse, hope, grief, and divorce. Love Beyond Love is her signature, she says, "Because to love as Christ loves, we must love beyond our natural perceptions of what love means, love beyond the hurt and the pain while giving love when it seems the hardest thing to do." She is a breast cancer survivor, a survivor of childhood sexual abuse, and a survivor of mental and emotional abuse. The books she has written and co-authored are To Touch the Hem of His Garment; My Journey Through Surviving Breast Cancer; Bling the Purpose, Pursuit, & Power of Women with Blind Faith Anthology; and Friendly Fire! Casualty of War in the Church. Prophetess Christine is an educator who has worked in higher education for more than twenty years. She has a master's degree in human services counseling -- marriage and family -- and is working on her doctoral degree.

Bowenchristine982@gmail.com
Christinebowen79@yahoo.com
RealTalkJust4Women@gmail.com
FACEBOOK: Christine J Bowen

CHAPTER 21

How to Build a Bridge and Get Over It

BY DOREETHA WHEATLEY

Love is patient. Love is kind. Love suffers long. Suffering long... I suffered so long for the sake of what I called love, never fully understanding the impact it would have on my five beautiful children as they watched me settle over and over and over again. They heard me say I was tired as they watched me take steps to walk away from a world of polygamy. They knew as much as I did as they heard me rant to anyone who would listen, adding to the shame they'd already endured because the family knew. I didn't know I was molding these children to believe what they should accept in their future relationships.

I made pleas for them to do better than I did as I told them my excuse that I didn't have anyone to tell me what I'm telling them. I told them what's acceptable and unacceptable as they watched me accept everything but what I truly wanted from their father. I caused them to have no trust in men and to be afraid to really love 100% without fear of heartbreak. I realized that I was also hurting myself. I'm getting it... someone's inability to accept my greatness has nothing to do with me. My heart had become black because I wanted love from a man not capable of giving it to me. I laid in the dark grave of uncultivated love formed from the lust of his own contention. I laid covered in the evidence of death. I held a faded memory of something buried with the regret of free will: love. Yet, I became a pistol to every woman who crossed the boundaries of holy matrimony. I attempted to exude strength a million times, only to end up back with the beautiful liar.

The women my husband had affairs with were homewrecking

whores in my mind, but one woman he had been seeing for years said something that resonated with me. "If it ain't me, it will be someone else, so why do you stay?" It still hurts today as I wonder why I stayed.

I attempted to make amends with those who wronged me because two wrongs don't make a right. Only to find it was useless because the other women never really left and his family...Well, lets just say blood is thicker than water so I had to forgive in my heart, because what they did wasn't personal, it was just their character. I had to choose to remove myself from those situations. People told me to leave, that I deserve better as I took my frustrations out on everyone who wasn't riding with me 100%. I was embarrassed as I constantly helped empower other women to love themselves first but couldn't make the mark myself. I was angry with my family when they didn't want to be around my husband. I often thought that misery loves company. But what if people really want what's best for you even if they don't have the strength to practice what they preach? After all, that's what I was doing. Through all of my confusion and attempts to forgive, I finally realized the pain was debilitating as I lay on my bed, realizing that two thirds of the day was gone, and I had done nothing productive. My body wouldn't let me; my mind was everywhere attempting to embrace the fear I had had for more than twenty years. What will I do now? My spirit was broken as I lay in a pit of deep hurt and frustration brought on by my inability to obey and my ability to love. How could he do this again? It would have been better for me to ask how I put myself in a position of demobilization again. But I told myself, sighing, that it's okay. Each sigh might not have been a relief but a release of the ties that bound. Each sigh brought another painful stitch as the healing process took place -- the mending of my heart. I closed my eyes and I sighed a release of being second fiddle, a release of settling and years of second guessing my womanhood, a release of confusion that God wasn't in, a release of codependency. I sighed and I released bottled tears that I thought dried up with his promises of no more tears. I cried, and I moaned as I grieved the perfect death of my love. My soul ached as it ripped apart once-mended souls, and I blew the very life of him into the heavens to give to God all I couldn't handle. I closed my eyes to erase the memories, to envision a brighter day. I breathed a sigh of relief as I was surrounded by those who love me unconditionally.

My name is Doreetha Reesie Wheatley. I am a designer dressmaker, sewing instructor, author, vision strategist, and owner of R.P. Couture's Boutique and Entrepreneurial Hub. I'm an entrepreneur who understands what love truly means and it enabled me to build this bridge over infidelity. Although I was beyond capable of loving others, I later realized that I didn't truly love myself. It's always been humorous to hear people say you need to leave or you need to love yourself more as they disregard your struggle or your frailties and tell you to get over it. Hunh? Get over it? I would find myself screaming *how*? What happens next? How do you actually begin the process of building a bridge to get over it?

According to Wikipedia, a bridge is a structure built to span a physical obstacle without blocking the way underneath. It is constructed for the purpose of providing passage over the obstacle, which is usually something that is otherwise difficult or impossible to cross. There you have it. We've recognized an obstacle that is obviously difficult or impossible to get over. So now we build a bridge. Although, this bridge or obstacle is often manifested physically, the bridges we need to build are for mental or emotional obstacles.

When it comes to building a bridge to get over infidelity, I had to first admit that it was a problem. After all admission is the first step to recovery. The problem usually starts with us because we try to control the actions of others, when in reality we can control only how we respond. How did I respond to his infidelity? I tried to change him. I sacrificed myself, my well being, and my self image in hopes that someone would behave differently. Well, my only job was to believe he was who he showed me he was *the first time*. I should've loved myself enough to do the right thing for my emotional well-being. I should have walked away.

What does that bridge to walk look like? It looks like seeking counseling. It looks like creating a plan to securely and safely exit. It takes imagining what peace and love look like. It looks like having a support system to help you gather the tools needed to get to the other side. It takes strength and constant reminders that you deserve better and believing you do. Once you've worked your way to the other side, you'll have a foundation strong enough to help others across that same obstacle. After my demobilizing moment I decided to write, I stopped caring about what people would say if I were totally transparent. I crushed mediocrity and made the decision to write as I walked myself and others through the twelve steps to recovery from infidelity.

Doreetha "Reesie" Wheatley

Doreetha "Reesie" Wheatley is a Chicago dressmaker, designer, author and vision strategist She specializes in garment making for special occasions and spends her time helping others' visions come alive through entrepreneurship. At the tender age of eight, she tapped into her God-given talent of sewing, with Barbie as her first client. She would use socks, mittens, and even aluminum foil to create garments so Barbie would stand out among her peers. She later began reconstructing her mom's old garments, making hats from leather and duplicating accessories from magazines. In high school, Reesie began designing and creating clothing using the skills acquired in fashion design class at Chicago Vocational High School. There, modeling for a local organization called Prom Connection paved the way to her passion for fashion and the desire to showcase her designs on the runway. But it didn't stop there, while running to class at this four block-long facility, she noticed the word entrepreneur plastered above a showcase of memoirs in the hallway. From that moment, she knew that was her call.

With an entrepreneurial spirit, immediately after graduating high school Reesie began creating Easter, wedding, and prom dresses. Word began to travel, and for the next thirty years, family and friends spread the word of her great talent and reasonable prices. After completing a sixteen week program with The Women's Self Employment Project, Reesie made her dream, Reesie's Pieces, a reality. With continual growth and the support of amazing designers who have trained and mentored Reesie, her business, Reesie's Pieces, has become a household name to many. She is now launching her ready-to-wear couture line, RP Couture, allowing women to look like a million without spending one. With Reesie there's never a "who wore it best," moment because her creations are high in demand but limited in supply.

Reesie has a passion for giving back. For several years, she promoted a buy-one-give-one sale of her full circle scarf, reflecting the belief that everything must come full circle. For every scarf purchased, another one of same design was created and given to someone less fortunate. She also donates food and offers prayer during the Christmas season. Throughout the years Reesie has lived by the motto "Give and it shall be given," which drew the attention of Dr. Quinton de'Alexander (now Chief Tamba Taylor), CEO and Founder of the We Dream in Color foundation. He honored Reesie at the foundation's annual humanitarian event, recognizing Reesie's having survived domestic violence

129

and overcome homelessness. She also donated funds to build the Chief Tamba Taylor playground for disadvantage communities in Liberia. While obtaining her degree in social work, Reesie focused on youth and volunteers her time to teach underprivileged young people about fashion and entrepreneurship. She works through organizations such as A Better Tomorrow, Our Youth, a community forum, and Chicago Public Schools, to name a few.

She recently opened a 7,500-square-foot boutique and entrepreneurial hub on the South Chicago Corridor, offering new business owners the opportunity to share work space and access resources for continual growth and development.

dawheatleyr@gmail.com
www.reesiespiecescouture.com
FACEBOOK: @ReesiesPiecesCouture
*INSTAGRAM: @rpCouture_*

Made in the USA
Middletown, DE
16 March 2022